ON THE COVER
Wood frog (*Rana sylvatica*). Sagamore Hill NHS provides an important core of protected wetland and forest habitat that allows for the continued survival of species such as the wood frog, which have declined throughout most of Long Island. Photograph by David Brotherton.

Inventory of Amphibians and Reptiles at Sagamore Hill National Historic Site

Natural Resource Report NPS/NCBN/NRTR—2010/379

Robert P. Cook

National Park Service
Cape Cod National Seashore
Wellfleet, MA 02667
Robert_Cook@nps.gov

David K. Brotherton and John L. Behler[1]

Department of Herpetology
Wildlife Conservation Society
Bronx Zoo
Bronx, NY 10460-1099
dkb4112@yahoo.com
[1]deceased

September 2010

U.S. Department of the Interior
National Park Service
Natural Resource Program Center
Fort Collins, Colorado

The National Park Service, Natural Resource Program Center publishes a range of reports that address natural resource topics of interest and applicability to a broad audience in the National Park Service and others in natural resource management, including scientists, conservation and environmental constituencies, and the public.

The Natural Resource Technical Report Series is used to disseminate results of scientific studies in the physical, biological, and social sciences for both the advancement of science and the achievement of the National Park Service mission. The series provides contributors with a forum for displaying comprehensive data that are often deleted from journals because of page limitations.

All manuscripts in the series receive the appropriate level of peer review to ensure that the information is scientifically credible, technically accurate, appropriately written for the intended audience, and designed and published in a professional manner.

This report received informal peer review by subject-matter experts who were not directly involved in the collection, analysis, or reporting of the data. Data in this report were collected and analyzed using methods based on established, peer-reviewed protocols and were analyzed and interpreted within the guidelines of the protocols.

Views, statements, findings, conclusions, recommendations, and data in this report do not necessarily reflect views and policies of the National Park Service, U.S. Department of the Interior. Mention of trade names or commercial products does not constitute endorsement or recommendation for use by the U.S. Government.

This report is available from (http://www.nps.gov/nero/science/) and the Natural Resource Publications Management website (http://www.nature.nps.gov/publications/NRPM).

Please cite this publication as:

NPS 419/105746, September 2010

Contents

Figures

Tables

Executive Summary

Under a National Park Service/Wildlife Conservation Society Cooperative Agreement, we inventoried amphibians and reptiles at Sagamore Hill NHS (SAHI) on Cove Neck, Oyster Bay, New York from March to September 2002. Six standard sampling methods were used; anuran calling surveys, egg mass counts, visual encounter surveys, coverboards, turtle traps, and minnow traps. We recorded animals encountered outside of standard surveys as incidental encounters.

Ten species were recorded, representing 91% (10/11) of the species known to be present historically at SAHI and 59% (10/17) of the species that may have occurred. Spotted salamander, wood frog, northern diamond-backed terrapin, and eastern garter snake were the most abundant species in each taxonomic group. In descending order, the most widespread species were eastern box turtle, wood frog, eastern garter snake, spring peeper, and all others. The only "listed" species was eastern box turtle (NY *Special Concern*). Visual encounter surveys recorded 8 of 10 species, followed by incidental encounters (7), minnow trap survey (3), egg mass count and turtle trap survey (2), anuran calling survey (1), and coverboards (0). Six species, accounting for 61.5% of all individuals recorded, were recorded in permanent pond, four in vernal pond (24.5%) and deciduous forest (4.7%), three (1.4%) in field and one (7.9%) on coastal beach. Two wetlands, Woodpile pond and Heron pond had the greatest numbers of species and individuals recorded at them, highlighting the importance of wetlands at SAHI to amphibians and reptiles. Yet, most species at SAHI are primarily terrestrial, spending most of the year in woodland and field habitats. Amphibians use wetlands at SAHI primarily for reproduction and conversely, the three species of aquatic turtles at SAHI require well drained, open uplands for nesting.

Because there was virtually no historic data, a comprehensive trend analysis was not possible. However, painted turtles have declined and there is reason to believe that snakes have also, due to regional urbanization impacts. Although the herpetofauna of SAHI has likely declined, another reason for its low species richness is simply its small size (83 acres) and relative lack of wetland habitats. It has only two small ponds, one of which (Heron pond) appears to be a relatively short hydroperiod vernal pond, and no riparian habitat.

Most of the species recorded at SAHI in 2002 are fairly common, suburban tolerant species. However, wood frog, spotted salamander, gray treefrog, and box turtle are locally uncommon species that generally do not survive well in urban-suburban landscapes. Given the impacts of urbanization on amphibians and reptiles, it is clear that the persistence of many species in suburbanized landscapes will be limited to landscapes where patches of several hundred acres of reasonably intact native habitat are present, generally with a park, preserve, or similar "greenspace" at its core. Cove Neck provides a landscape of relatively low density suburban development with much of the native vegetation still intact and SAHI as the core of protected habitat needed to support populations of box turtles and other native amphibians and reptiles in what is the least urbanized corner of Nassau County. However, park management needs to be vigilant for external threats and should ensure that the mowing necessary to maintain the cultural landscape is done without impacting box turtles and other species using field and pasture habitat.

Acknowledgments

Funding for this project was provided by the National Park Service, and numerous people assisted with the project. Charlie Eichelberger and Linh Phu spent countless hours in the field at all hours of the day and night, organized and summarized the data gathered, and provided summaries of their findings. Scott Gurney of SAHI was especially helpful with his insight into the land use history of the park, and in identifying important habitats likely to support amphibians and reptiles. Amy Verone also provided important insight into site history and historic documents.

We are also grateful to Al Lindberg, Jeremy Feinberg, Norm Soule, and Peter Warney for sharing their notes, data, and observations of the herpetofauna in and around SAHI and elsewhere on Long Island.

Preliminary drafts of this report were improved as a result of critical review and comments by Scott Gurney and Dennis Skidds, who also provide GIS and map support. Special thanks to Robin Baranowski for final formatting.

Introduction

Sagamore Hill (SAHI), is an 83 acre (34.6 ha) historic site on the north shore of Nassau County, Long Island, that was the home and estate of President Theodore Roosevelt. Located on a small peninsula known as Cove Neck, in Oyster Bay, New York, SAHI contains Roosevelt's home and associated cultural landscape, historic buildings, and archeological resources. It was established as a National Historic Site in 1962 through a donation and endowment to the National Park Service (NPS) by the Theodore Roosevelt Association.

In 1998, a Cooperative Agreement between the National Park Service and the Wildlife Conservation Society was formed to assess amphibian and reptile populations at parks within the Northeast Region of the National Park Service. While the goals of the project vary between parks, they generally are as follows:

- Inventory and record at least 90% of the species currently estimated to occur in the park.

- Determine the occurrence and status of species of management concern (e.g., state and federal *Threatened, Endangered,* and *Special Concern Species,* and other declining species).

- Determine abundance categories, distribution, and habitat use of documented species.

- Identify critical habitats of *Threatened, Endangered,* and *Special Concern* species.

- Provide basis for future development of a long term monitoring program.

- Analyze species occurrence against historical occurrence and evaluate the state of the park's herpetofauna, on a site and regional scale.

Determining what species were historically present at SAHI was a difficult and uncertain process. Although the writings of Roosevelt and other family members make some references to the amphibians and reptiles they encountered at SAHI (Bellavia and Curry 1995), this only provided information on a couple of species. Although SAHI staff have observed some species here, there have been no prior surveys of amphibians and reptiles and only one known published reference to any amphibian and reptile found at SAHI, a ring-necked snake (*Diadophis punctatus edwardsii*) found by Burnley (1968). In contrast to the lack of SAHI-specific data, the herpetofauna of Long Island was well documented over the course of the 20th century. Schlauch (1974) mapped the distribution of amphibians and reptiles on Long Island based on historic museum specimens and published records, and observations made by reliable naturalists in the 1960's and 1970's. Although SAHI was not a focus of this work, it shows the occurrence of many species in the vicinity of SAHI. Similarly, Schlauch (1978) divided Nassau County into 18 tracts and detailed the "recent" occurrence of species within each. The northeastern tract, where SAHI occurs, had 18 species recorded. SAHI occurs within the Bayville and Lloyd Harbor USGS topographic map quadrangles, and more recently (1990-2007), a total of 16 native species were recorded in them by the New York State Herp Atlas Project (Breisch and Ozard, in prep). In addition, 24 species have been recorded at Muttontown preserve (Lindberg 1994), a 550 acre (229 ha) nature preserve approximately seven km southwest of SAHI. Given that the range and

1

abundance of native species on Long Island is declining not expanding, we assumed any current or recent record to also indicate historic occurrence. Thus, based on all these sources, a total of 29 species historically occurred in the general vicinity of SAHI (Table 1). However, SAHI is a couple of orders of magnitude smaller than the "general vicinity" and given its small size and limited habitat diversity, it is unlikely that it ever supported all these species. Therefore, a more realistic estimate of the "historic" herpetofauna was generated by excluding those species which we felt did not have adequate habitat, given what we know about their habitat needs and the landscape and its history (Bellavia and Curry 1995). For example, although the Northern cricket frog occurred in Oyster Bay near Sagamore Hill (Smith et al. 1995), cricket frogs bred in open, grassy marshes (Overton 1914, Gibbs et al. 2007), a habitat type not present at Sagamore Hill. Based on this approach, we estimate that the historic herpetofauna of SAHI and adjacent Cove Neck may have included 17 species, and the known historic herpetofauna consisted of 11 species (Table 1).

Given the uniform lack of information on SAHI's herpetofauna, the target species of this inventory was the complete suite of possibly-occurring species. Because these are broad in terms of taxonomic groups and habitat affinities, the inventory employed six standardized methods in a variety of habitats. Incidental encounters were also recorded to provide additional information on species presence and distribution. The habitat type of all sites where amphibians and reptiles were found was described, and the species and the habitat types they occupied were analyzed.

Table 1. Estimated historic herpetofauna of SAHI, based on records of amphibians and reptiles from Sagamore Hill and vicinity. Of the 29 species known to be present in the local species pool, the 17 in bold may have occurred on Cove Neck and at SAHI, given the habitats present. The 11 species with an asterisk (*) are known to have occurred historically at SAHI.

Species	Schlauch 1978a	Lindberg 1994	Roosevelt Archives	Current Survey	NYS DEC Herp Atlas
Spotted salamander*	X	X		X	
Marbled salamander		X			
Eastern tiger salamander	X	X			
Red-spotted newt		X			
Eastern red-backed salamander*	X	X		X	X
Northern two-lined salamander	X				X
Eastern spadefoot toad		X			
Fowler's toad	X	X			X
Northern cricket frog		X			
Spring peeper*	X	X		X	X
Gray treefrog*	X	X		X	X
Northern green Frog	X	X			X
American bullfrog	X	X			X
Wood frog*	X	X		X	X
Southern leopard frog					X
Pickerel frog	X				X
Snapping turtle*	X	X		X	X
Painted turtle*	X	X	X	X	X
Spotted turtle		X			
Eastern box turtle*	X	X		X	X
Northern diamond-backed terrapin*				X	X
Northern water snake		X			
Northern brown snake		X			X
Eastern garter snake*	X	X		X	X
Eastern ribbon snake		X			
Eastern milk snake		X			
Northern ring-necked snake*	X	X			
Northern red-bellied snake	X				
Northern black racer	X	X			

Study Area

Purchased by Theodore Roosevelt to be his home in 1880, Sagamore Hill estate originally consisted of 155 acres on Cove Neck, one of the many "necks" in this region that project into Long Island sound. Although Roosevelt sold 68 acres soon after his purchase, he maintained his 87 acres as a working farm with fields, pastures, an orchard, woodlands and beach, on Cold Spring Harbor. Woodlands such as these presumably were the dominant plant community on Cove Neck prior to clearing for agriculture. The estate was divided into areas that varied in the intensity of manipulation, and woodlands and beach comprised 32 acres. There were also two freshwater ponds. Woodpile pond was a small, permanent pond north of the gardens that received runoff from the garden and pig-pen. Heron Pond, aka Lower Lake, was a vernal pond in the woods above Cold Spring Harbor. Roosevelt also noted the existence of a spring, known as "Frog Spring" somewhere along his north eastern boundary. In addition to these freshwater wetlands, the eastern part of the estate was bounded on the east by Cold Spring Harbor and inter-tidal flats, with a low beachgrass-dominated sand spit, Eel Creek and salt marsh habitat immediately to the west. Following Roosevelt's death in 1919, the amount of agricultural activity began to decline and by the late 1940's it ended. As a result some open field and pasture habitat succeeded into shrub and early successional stage woodland (Bellavia and Curry 1995).

At the time of this survey, SAHI consisted of 83 acres that, in addition to buildings, roads, and parking lots, were a mixture of lawns, fields, orchard, successional woodlands, and the older, more mature woodlands, salt marsh, and beach east of Old Orchard. These latter habitats are little changed since Roosevelt's time. The two freshwater ponds, Woodpile pond and Heron pond are also still extant, but "Frog Spring" no longer exists. Although in Nassau County, a county that defined the post World War II suburbanization boom, SAHI is in the least urbanized portion of the county (Schlauch 1978a) and the adjoining landscape is dominated by low density residential development, with significant amounts of native-dominated woodland and lesser amounts of open lawn.

Methods

Sampling Overview

We sampled SAHI with a three person crew as part of an effort to survey the herpetofauna of three NPS units over the course of the 2002 field season. Because the herpetofauna of the northeast United States consists of a variety of species, each with differing periods of activity (which can also vary somewhat annually), we distributed sampling effort over the course of the spring and summer activity season. Given this, and the logistics of sampling three separate NPS units on Long Island (SAHI; William Floyd Estate NHS; Fire Island NS) we sampled them in bouts that varied in duration in proportion to their size and presumed faunal/zoogeographic complexity. Over the course of a month the crew sampled one and then moved on to the next, such that a full round of sampling was conducted each month during the months of April, May, June, August, and September. For SAHI, each monthly sampling bout was generally one week long.

The general approach of sampling was to balance the need for standardized methods and quantifiable results with the primary goal of determining species presence. Since amphibians and reptiles found at SAHI are variable in habitat use and seasonal patterns of detectability, we employed a number of methods, both general and habitat/taxa specific. These were; Anuran Calling Surveys (ACS), Egg Mass Counts (EMC), Coverboard Surveys (CB), Turtle Trap Surveys (TTS), Minnow Trap Surveys (MTS), Habitat or Area-specific Visual-encounter Surveys (VES), and Incidental Encounters (IE). We employed general methods (i.e. VES) across all habitats for the entire field season, whereas habitat/taxa specific methods were employed at those times of the year when the target species/habitat are known to be most efficiently sampled.

The combination of methods chosen recognized that multiple methods were necessary to detect the wide range of potentially-occurring species and that some species are difficult to detect due to rarity or behavior. Thus, a degree of redundancy was needed to increase the likelihood of encountering these rare/hard to find species, most all of which were "target species". Collectively, the methods we employed were designed to provide a comprehensive list of species occurrence and a reasonable estimate of relative abundance and habitat use. The park was divided into 20 "zones" delineated in the Cultural Landscape Report (Bellavia and Curry 1995) and the 1996 Vegetation Survey (Stalter 1996) and sites for standardized surveys were selected from these. Site selection for standardized surveys was designed to sample across the range of habitat types present as well as to be spatially balanced, and given the park's small size, nearly all upland "zones" were sampled (Table 2, Figure 1). Similarly, because the number of ponds and wetlands were limited, all were sampled. We divided habitats into two categories, wetland or upland, and further sub-divided these into more specific habitat types: permanent pond, temporary pond, salt marsh; coastal beach, field, deciduous forest.

Table 2. Overview of standardized survey sites and sampling methods used at each.

Sample Site	Habitat Type	Calling Survey	Egg Mass Count	Visual Encounter Survey	Cover Board	Turtle Trap Survey	Minnow Trap Survey
Woodpile Pond	permanent pond	X	X	X		X	X
Heron Pond	vernal pond	X	X	X		X	X
CSH Beach	coastal beach			X			
Eel Creek Salt Marsh	salt marsh			X		X	
The Pasture	field			X	X		
Old Barn	field			X	X		
The Field	field			X	X		
Old Orchard	field				X		
Upland-Salt Marsh Edge	field				X		
WestSlope/Punchbowl	deciduous forest			X	X		
Cousin Beech Woods	deciduous forest			X	X		
Heron Pond Woods	deciduous forest			X	X		
Rifle Pit/South Slope	deciduous forest			X			

8

Marking, Measurement, and Aging/Sexing of Captured Animals

Captured animals were treated differently in terms of marking and measurements, with exact details determined by whether a species was a "target" species, as well as the inherent ability to mark a species. While several different methods were employed to capture/sample animals, details of marking and measuring were based on details of species, not method of capture.

We classified amphibians as larvae or adult-form, and adult-form individuals into age categories (metamorph, juvenile, adults) but did not mark, measure, or weigh them. We measured snakes' snout-vent length (SVL), total length (TL), and mass, and sexed them based on degree of tail contour (Conant and Collins 1998), but did not mark them. We marked all turtles for individual identification, with each given a unique set of notches in the marginal scutes, using a code system modified from Cagle (1939). For all turtles captured, we measured carapace length (CL), carapace width (CW), plastron length (PL), and mass. Turtles were sexed based on external features for each species described in Ernst et al. (1994). Individuals were classified as adult, as opposed to juvenile, based on the following size criteria: snapping turtles, males with CL >210 mm and females with CL>200 mm (Congdon et al. 1987, 1992, Ernst et al. 1994); box turtles CL>120 mm (Dodd 2001). In painted turtles, we sexed males based on the presence of elongated foreclaws and a long thick tail, with the anal opening posterior to the carapace margin (Ernst et al. 1994). Zweifel (1989) found that elongation of toenails occurred in Long Island, NY, males as small as 76 mm PL and in most, if not all males, by 90 mm PL. Thus, we classified any painted turtle >90 mm PL and lacking male secondary sexual characteristics as a female (Zweifel 1989). Based on Long Island, NY, data (Zweifel 1989), males with PL>80mm and females with PL>110 mm were considered adults.

Anuran Calling Surveys

Anuran calling surveys (ACS) were conducted using the Wisconsin frog and toad survey method (Heyer et al. 1994). ACS records the presence of species calling at specific sites and provides an index of abundance based on the calling intensity. Call index (CI) values and criteria for assigning them are; 0 = no calls, 1 = individuals can be counted (no overlapping of calls), 2 = overlapping of calls (can still be counted), 3 = full chorus-calls are constant and individually indistinguishable. The surveyors arrived at each sample site at least one half-hour after dusk. Surveyors listened for anuran calls for five minutes, recording species heard, the number of individuals heard, if any, and the call index for each species.

We surveyed SAHI's two wetlands, Woodpile pond and Heron pond four times between April 15 and June 11, 2002.

Egg Mass Counts

Amphibians such as spotted salamanders and wood frogs (*Rana sylvatica*) migrate to ponds in early spring to breed, depositing gelatinous egg masses attached to fallen tree branches and vegetation in the water (Petranka 1998).We used egg mass counts (Cook and Boland 2005) to determine presence of these species and obtain an estimate of breeding effort. In these counts, the observer traversed the entire pond, searching for, identifying, and counting all egg masses observed. We counted egg masses at SAHI's two wetlands, Woodpile pond and Heron pond, on two occasions, 3/25/02 and 4/12/02.

Visual Encounter Surveys

We conducted visual encounter surveys (VES) (Crump and Scott 1994) in all habitats likely to support amphibians and reptiles, i.e. ponds, salt marsh, beach, woodland, and field. Each wetland or upland VES area (Figure 1) was searched thoroughly and time taken to do so recorded. Searchers used an approach intended to maximize the numbers and diversity of captures by moving through the area and searching under the best available cover (e.g. logs, boards, metal debris) favored by amphibians and reptiles (Bury and Raphael 1983), and by dip netting ponds (Heyer et al. 1994). Although the original plans called for sites within each habitat type to be sampled the same number of times, this was not always the case. We standardized results of VES as a capture rate (CR) for each species, calculated by dividing the total number of individuals recorded by the total search effort (person hours) spent for each search. Person hours are the total amount of time spent searching, multiplied by the number of people participating in the search.

Upland VES

Nine upland areas encompassing coastal beach, woodland, and field habitats were surveyed. Cold Spring Harbor Beach was surveyed on seven occasions from 3/36/02 to 9/9/02, for a total of 8.0 search hours.

We searched four deciduous forest areas six or seven times each between 26 March and 9 September 2002. Start and end times, number of searchers, and the identification, and number of individuals found were recorded. Sampling effort is detailed below.

   Woodland survey sites were:
   1. Cousin Beech Woods – seven surveys, 10.4 total search hours.
   2. Heron Pond Woods – six surveys, 8.3 total search hours.
   3. Rifle Pit/South Slope- six surveys, 8.9 total search hours.
   4. West Slope/Punch Bowl- six surveys, 8.8 total search hours.

We searched four fields five times between 16 April and 10 September 2002. Start and end times, number of searchers, and the identification and number of individuals found were recorded. Sampling effort is detailed below.

   Field survey sites were:
   1. Old Barn - 5 surveys, 1.9 total search hours.
   2. Old Orchard – 5 surveys, 3.8 total search hours.
   3. The Field – 5 surveys, 3.7 total search hours.
   4. The Pasture – 5 surveys, 3.9 total search hours.

Wetland VES

We searched ponds by traversing the entire pond, sampling with a dip-net for amphibian larvae and adults, as well as turtles and snakes. Start and end times, number of searchers, and the identification, and number of individuals found were recorded. Woodpile pond was searched on five occasions, for a total of 5.3 search hours, between 16 April and 11 September 2002. Heron Pond was not searched in April due to a lack of water. We searched Heron Pond three times, for a total of 0.9 search hours, between 15 May and 11 September 2002. 28 March and 18 September 2002. Eel creek salt marsh was surveyed six times for a total of 4.9 hours between 16 April and 11 September 2002.

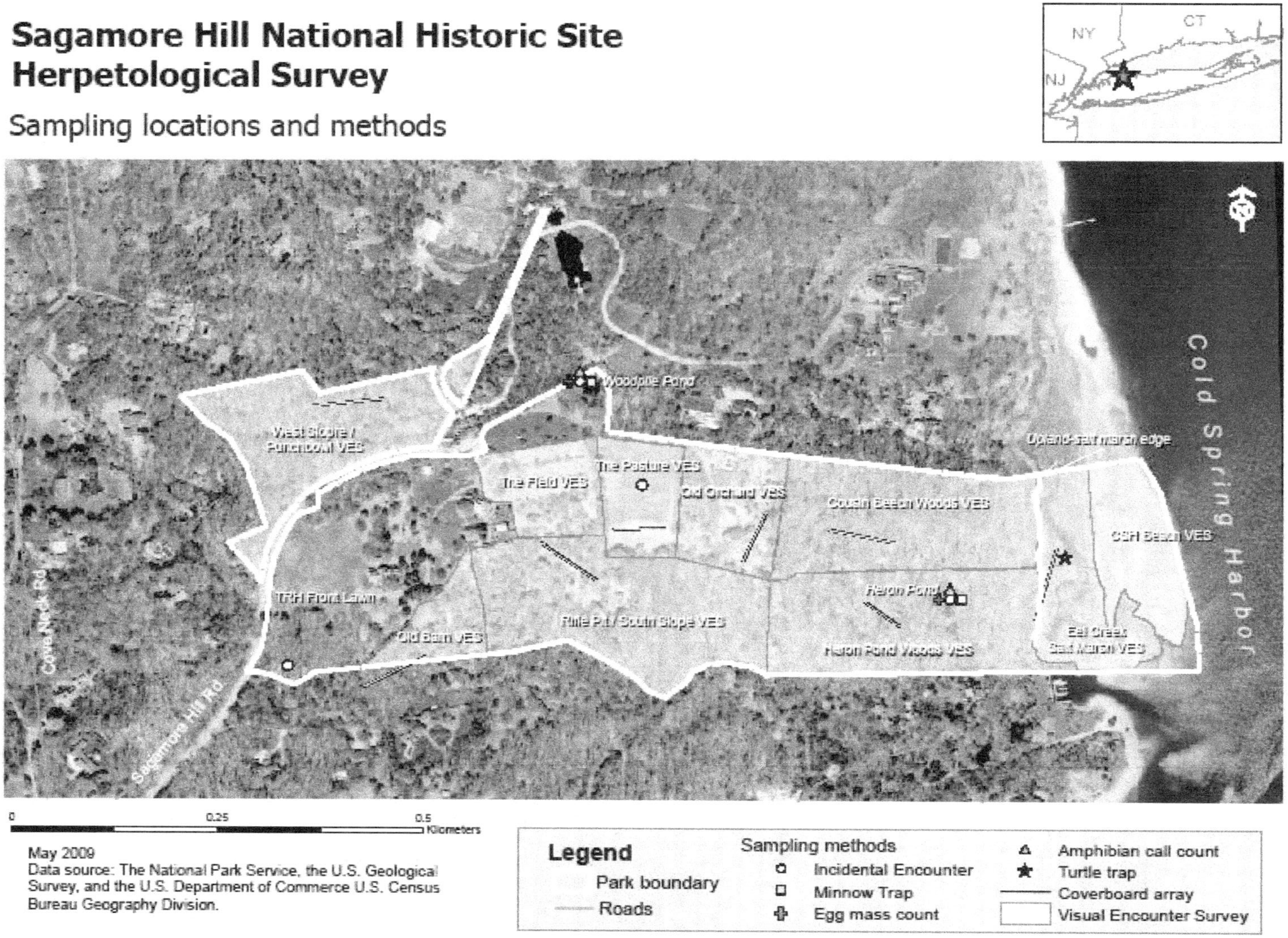

Sagamore Hill National Historic Site
Herpetological Survey
Sampling locations and methods
NY
CT
NJ
Cold Spring Harbor
Woodpile Pond
West Slope / Punchbowl VES
The Field VES
The Pasture VES
Old Orchard VES
Cousin Beach Woods VES
Upland-salt marsh edge
CSH Beach VES
Heron Pond
Heron Pond Woods VES
Eel Creek Salt Marsh VES
Rifle Pit / South Slope VES
TRH Front Lawn
Old Barn VES
Cove Neck Rd
Sagamore Hill Rd
0
0.25
0.5
Kilometers
May 2009
Data source: The National Park Service, the U.S. Geological Survey, and the U.S. Department of Commerce U.S. Census Bureau Geography Division.
Legend
Park boundary
Roads
Sampling methods
Incidental Encounter
Minnow Trap
Egg mass count
Amphibian call count
Turtle trap
Coverboard array
Visual Encounter Survey

Figure 1. Location of sampling sites and visual encounter survey areas used in herpetofaunal inventory at Sagamore Hill, 2002.

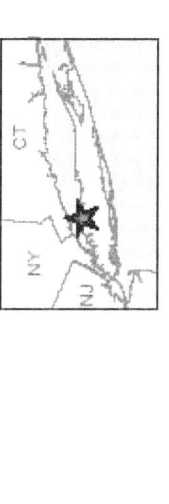

Coverboards

We used coverboards (Grant et al. 1992) primarily to inventory snakes, but they were also expected to detect terrestrial amphibians. Boards were 0.6 m x 1.2 m (2' x 4') and made of corrugated sheet metal or plywood. In March 2002, coverboards were deployed at four woodland sites(Cousin Beech Woods, Heron Pond Woods, West Slope/Punchbowl) and five field sites (Old Barn, Old Orchard, The Field, The Pasture, Upland Marsh Edge) (Figure 1). We placed eight boards five meters apart in linear "arrays" consisting of alternating wood and metal boards. We checked coverboards twice/month in April and August, and once in May, June, and July. Thus each array had a total of seven visits and 56 board checks.

We calculated a capture rates (CR) as the number of snake captures under boards divided by the total number of board checks for each site. Each time a board was checked constituted a "board check". Therefore, a site with eight boards visited six times equaled 48 board checks. The number of snake captures per 100 coverboard checks was calculated as:

$$CR = \frac{(\#\,of\,snake\,captures)}{(total\,\#\,of\,board\,checks)} \times 100$$

Turtle Trap Surveys

We used welded-wire crab traps measuring 30.5cm x 30.5cm x 60.1cm (12"x12"x 24"), with a mesh size of 1.3cm x 2.5cm (0.5" x 1") to sample shallow areas for small aquatic/semi-aquatic turtles such as spotted turtles (*Clemmys guttata*). We used funnel traps made of D-shaped metal hoops and 2.6cm (1") nylon mesh to sample deeper pond areas for aquatic turtles such as painted (*Chrysemys picta*) and snapping turtles (*Chelydra serpentina*) (Harless and Morlock 1989). Two to five traps, baited with sardines in vegetable oil and checked daily, were set for three-day periods between 15 April and 13 June 2002 at three sites. Each turtle captured was assigned a unique, individual identification number and, using a three-sided file, triangular notches were made on marginal scutes to represent that number (Cagle 1939).

Trap sites were:
1. Woodpile Pond – (3, 2 to 3 day trapping periods, 2 to 5 traps, 31 trap nights total)
2. Heron Pond – (3, 3-day trapping periods, 5 traps, 45 trap nights total)
3. Eel Creek – (2, 3-day trapping periods, 5 traps, 30 trap nights total)

Minnow Trap Surveys

We used wire mesh minnow traps measuring 15.2 cm x 15.2 cm x 30.5 cm (6"x 6"x 12") to sample Woodpile Pond and Heron Pond for adult and larval salamanders, adult and larval anurans, and aquatic snakes (Heyer et al. 1994) between 15 April and 16 August 2002. Each pond was sampled in April, May, June, and August for three nights with four traps, for a total effort of 48 trap nights. Since this method primarily captures amphibians, which were not marked for individual recognition, abundance was quantified as total captures (rather than unique individuals) per 100 trap nights.

Incidental Encounters

Any encounter with an amphibian or reptile not recorded as data in one of the standardized surveys was considered an incidental encounter. We recorded these to augment data collected during formal surveys, including credible observations made by park staff and visitors. For each incidental encounter, species, life stage, method of documentation, as well as location, habitat, and UTM coordinates were recorded, though some of these data were sometimes missing from visitor reports.

Quantifying Abundance and Distribution

Quantifying actual abundance of the species encountered was not possible for a number of reasons. The methods we used generally did not estimate actual population size, but rather provided a method-specific index of abundance, such as a capture rate (catch per unit effort). In addition, each of the six methods provided a sample possibly biased towards a particular species or group of species or sex. Although sampling effort was divided among the different methods in an attempt to compensate for possible sampling bias, the amount of sampling bias, the extent to which the use of different methods may have balanced this bias, and the influence of other covariates, such as habitat type and breeding habits, were not estimated.

We derived an index of overall abundance for each species by summing the number of adult form individuals or equivalents encountered during each of the six survey methods. For visual encounter surveys, coverboard checks, turtle and minnow traps, and incidental encounters, the numbers of adult form individuals of a given species encountered during each sampling occasion were summed. Turtle shells (carapace/plastron), snake skins, and reptile nests were also considered to represent one adult individual. Because anuran calling surveys do not directly count adults, index values were converted to conservative estimates of the number of calling males present, based on data collected at Cape Cod National Seashore where both index values and estimates of numbers calling were made (Cook, unpublished data). Conservatively estimated numbers are as follows: gray treefrog (*Hyla versicolor*) Index 1=3 males; spring peeper (*Pseudacris crucifer*) Index 1=3 males, Index 2=7 males, Index 3=20 males. Estimates of calling male anurans do not include those females that may be present. Because egg mass counts do not directly count adults, the numbers of females represented was estimated as follows. For spotted salamanders (*Ambystoma maculatum*), Cook (1978) determined that, on average, each egg mass represented 0.633 females. Thus, the number of females present at a site was estimated as 0.633 times the number of egg masses. For wood frog egg mass counts, each egg mass represents one adult female (Crouch and Paton 2000). For wood frog larvae, because egg masses contain ca. 1000 embryos on average (Redmer and Trauth 2005) we conservatively considered that larvae up to 1000 represented one female. Because we did not mark amphibians, for the purposes of estimating an overall index of abundance, we also treated reptiles as though they had not been marked.

Although the total numbers recorded for each species provide an index of overall abundance, it is an uncalibrated index, and its relationship to actual abundance is unknown. These numbers, and their derivatives, are best viewed as indicating the order of magnitude of a species' abundance and providing a reasonably accurate representation of relative and ranked abundance within each taxonomic group (i.e. frogs/toads, turtles, snakes). Although these numbers are of value for some inter-specific comparisons and community analysis, and are likely accurate in identifying abundant versus rare species, differences between species whose index of abundance are of the same order of magnitude may not reflect true differences in abundance.

Incidental encounters represent occasions when animals were encountered outside of formal standardized surveys. Such occasions include when a species that is not the target of a given survey method is encountered during a standard survey, such as when an amphibian is observed while checking a turtle trap. Thus incidental encounters may occur at sites where standardized surveys were conducted, but often occur at other locations in the park. A measure of a species' overall distribution was obtained by combining the number of standardized survey sites and incidental encounter locations at which it was recorded. This summed term is referred to as "localities". There were 14 localities. Of these, 13 were standardized survey sites, four were standardized survey sites at which incidental encounters also occurred, and one was an incidental encounter location only

Data Management
Common and scientific names and spellings are those of Crother et al. (2000, 2003). A Garmin III Plus Global Positioning System (GPS) unit was used to record the distance or area searched during time-constrained surveys and the coordinates of coverboard arrays (Appendix C). Coordinates of each site surveyed during standardized surveys and location identified during incidental encounters were also recorded. GPS locality data were recorded as Universal Transverse Mercator (UTM) (zone 18N) grid coordinates X=x-axis or Easting, and Y=y-axis or Northing, using NAD83.

Data collected in the course of this study, original data sheets, and voucher photos are archived with the National Park Service, Northeast Coastal and Barrier Inventory and Monitoring Network at the University of Rhode Island (http://science.nature.nps.gov/im/units/ncbn/).

Results

Overview of Park Herpetofauna

We recorded a total of 10 species, five amphibians (two salamander and three anuran) and five reptiles (four turtle and one snake). Of the 278 individuals recorded, 82% were amphibians and 18% were reptiles. By taxonomic group, frogs comprised 74.8% of all individuals, turtles 16.9%, salamanders 7.2%, and snakes 1.1%. The most abundant species in each taxonomic group, based on total numbers recorded, were spotted salamander (*Ambystoma maculatum*), wood frog (*Rana sylvatica*), northern diamond-backed terrapin (*Malaclemys t. terrapin*), and eastern garter snake (*Thamnophis s. sirtalis*) (Table 3).

Animals were recorded from 10 of 14 (71%) locations (13 standardized survey sites plus 1 incidental encounter location) (Figures 2, 3, 4). Based on frequency of occurrence, the most widespread species in each taxonomic group was eastern box turtle (6 or 43% of all localities), wood frog (4 or 29%), eastern garter snake (3 or 21%), and spotted salamander and eastern red-backed salamander (1 or 7.1%; Table 4). The most species rich site was Woodpile Pond, with six species recorded, followed by Heron Pond (4 species) and West Slope/Punchbowl (3 species) (Table 5, Figure 6). Woodpile Pond and Heron Pond also accounted for the greatest number of individuals recorded, 61.5% and 24.5%, respectively. The majority of these individuals were wood frogs and spring peepers (Table 5).

By habitat, the number of individuals recorded was greatest in wetlands (239/278 or 86% of individuals recorded) as was species richness (8 of 10 species) (Table 3, Figure 5). Within the six habitat sub-categories, species richness was greatest in permanent pond (6 species), followed by vernal pond and deciduous forest (4 species each), field (3 species), and coastal beach (1 species). No species were recorded in salt marsh habitat (Table 3).

Survey Methods Summary

Visual encounter surveys detected the greatest number of species, eight of 10, produced the only records of eastern red-backed salamander and northern diamond-backed terrapin and more records of eastern box turtle than any other method (Tables 6 and 7). In terms of individuals recorded, it was the second-most productive method, accounting for 30.9% of all captures (Table 7). Incidental encounters detected the second greatest number of species, seven, produced the only record of gray treefrog, the most records of painted turtle and garter snake, and 12.2% of all captures. Egg mass counts recorded more individuals than any other method (36.7%), accounted for most wood frogs, and detected two species. Anuran calling surveys detected only one species, spring peeper, and was the third most productive method, accounting for 15.5% of all individuals recorded (Table 7). Minnow trap surveys and turtle trap surveys produced moderate numbers of species and individuals, 3 and 4% and 2 and 0.7% respectively, and relatively moderate numbers of the species detected (Table 7). No amphibians or reptiles were detected in coverboard surveys.

Sagamore Hill National Historic Site Herpetological Survey

Amphibian Species Locations

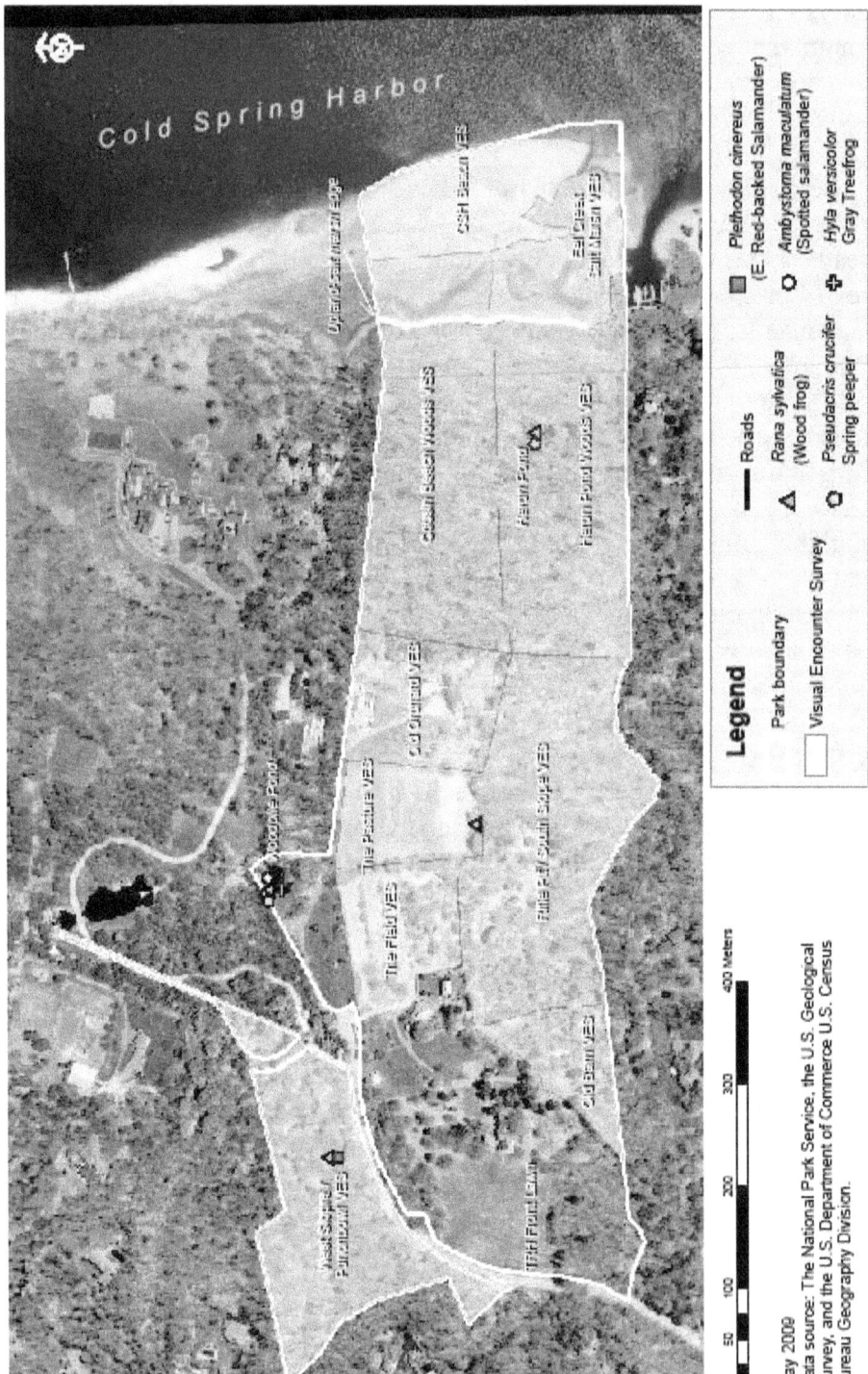

Figure 2. Location of amphibian detections at Sagamore Hill.

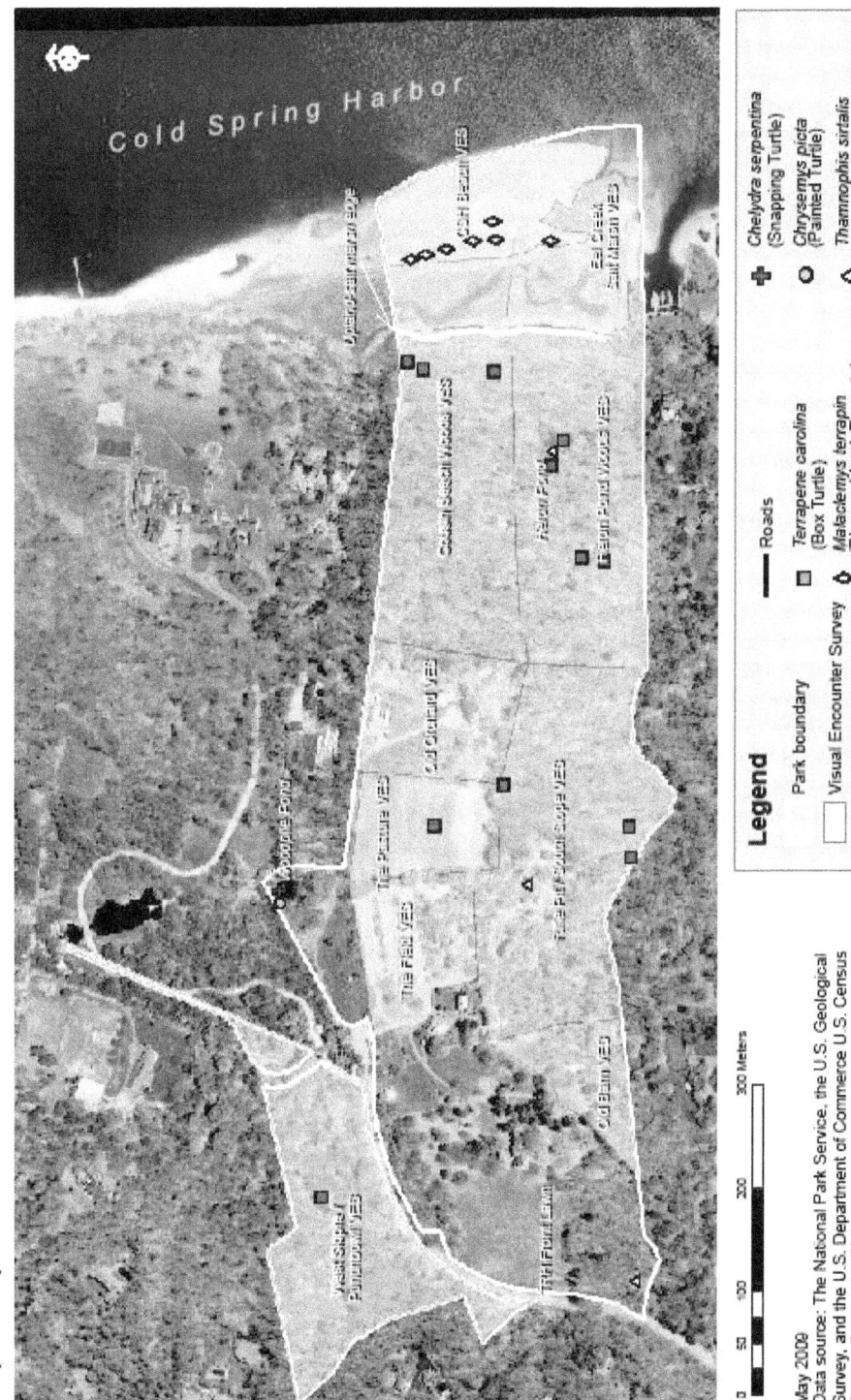

Figure 3. Location of reptile detections at Sagamore Hill.

Sagamore Hill National Historic Site
Herpetological Survey

Species Richness

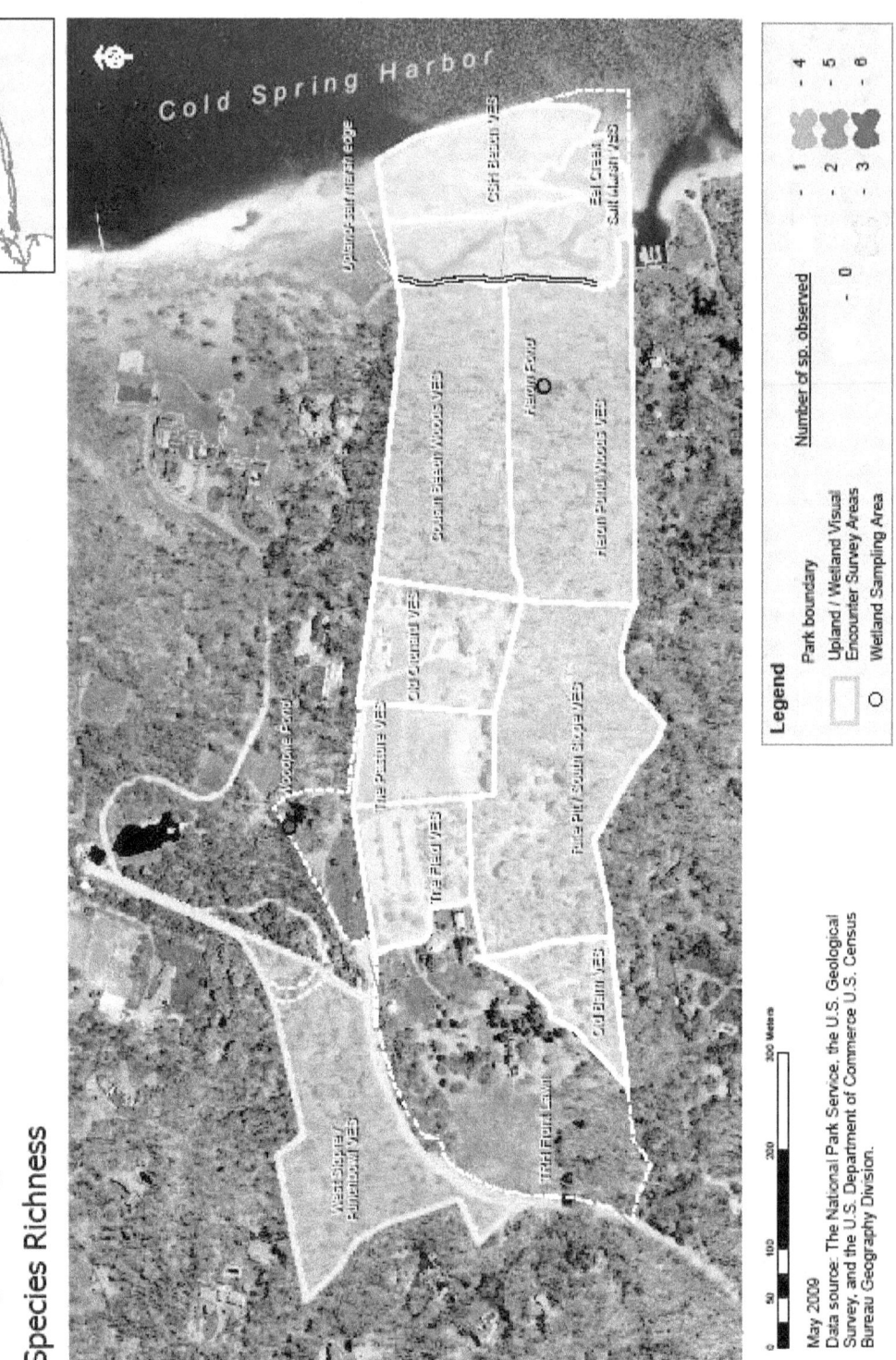

Figure 4. Species richness of areas sampled for amphibians and reptiles at Sagamore Hill.

Table 3. Number of adult form amphibian and reptile captures recorded during all surveys by habitat category at Sagamore Hill. Data include turtle shells and nests, and adult equivalents of egg masses and larvae. Relative abundance (RA) within taxonomic groups is the total number of a species recorded divided by total number recorded within each group (order), expressed as a percentage.

Species	Wetland			Upland			Total	RA (%) (Rank)
	Permanent pond	Vernal pond	Salt marsh	Coastal beach	Field	Deciduous forest		
Salamanders								
Spotted salamander	18						18	90.0 (1)
Eastern red-backed salamander						2	2	10.0 (2)
Frogs								
Spring peeper	67	28					95	45.7 (2)
Gray treefrog	2						2	1.0 (3)
Wood frog	74	35			1	1	111	53.4 (1)
Turtles								
Snapping turtle	4						4	8.5 (4)
Painted turtle	6						6	12.8 (3)
Northern diamond-backed terrapin				22			22	46.8 (1)
Eastern box turtle		4			2	9	15	31.9 (2)
Snakes								
Eastern garter snake		1			1	1	3	100 (1)
Total	171	68	0	22	4	13	278	
% of Total	61.5%	24.5%	0.0%	7.9%	1.4%	4.7%	100.0%	
Total # of Species	6	4 (8)	0	1	3	4 (5)		

(Wetland group Total # of Species: 8; Upland group Total # of Species: 5)

19

Table 4. Distribution by habitat category of amphibians and reptiles recorded at Sagamore Hill. Table entries indicate number of localities at which a species was recorded. Frequency of Occurrence (FO) is total number of localities a species was recorded from divided by total number (14). Number of localities includes both standardized survey sites (13) and incidental encounter locations (1).

Species	Wetland			Upland			Total	FO
	Permanent pond	Vernal pond	Salt marsh	Coastal beach	Field	Deciduous forest		
Salamanders								
Spotted salamander	1						1	7.1%
Eastern red-backed salamander						1	1	7.1%
Frogs								
Spring peeper	1	1					2	14.3%
Gray treefrog	1						1	7.1%
Wood frog	1	1			1	1	4	28.6%
Turtles								
Snapping turtle	1						1	7.1%
Painted turtle	1						1	7.1%
Northern diamond-backed terrapin				1			1	7.1%
Eastern box turtle		1			1	4	6	42.9%
Snakes								
Eastern garter snake		1			1	1	3	21.4%
# of Localities Sampled	1	1	1	1	5	5	14	

20

Table 5. Number of captures and total number of species recorded (S) at each of 13 standardized surveys sites and 1 incidental encounter location at Sagamore Hill. Species totals include all adult form individuals, plus nests (N), turtle shells (S), and adult equivalents of egg masses and larvae. Frequency of Occurrence (FO) is number of localities at which a species was recorded divided by total number of localities (14).

	Spotted Salamander	E. red-backed salamander	Spring peeper	Gray treefrog	Wood frog	Snapping turtle	Painted turtle	N. diamond-backed terrapin	Eastern box turtle	Eastern garter snake	Total	% of Total	S
Standardized Survey Sites													
Woodpile Pond	18		67	2	74	4	6				171	61.5%	6
Heron Pond			28		35				4	1	68	24.5%	4
CSH Beach								22			22	7.9%	1
Eel Creek Salt Marsh											0	0.0%	0
The Pasture					1				2		3	1.1%	2
Old Barn											0	0.0%	0
The Field										1	1	0.4%	1
Old Orchard											0	0.0%	0
Upland-salt Marsh Edge											0	0.0%	0
West Slope/Punchbowl		2			1				1		4	1.4%	3
Cousin Beech Woods									3		3	1.1%	1
Heron Pond Woods									3		3	1.1%	1
Rifle Pit/South Slope									2		2	0.7%	1
Incidental Encounter Location													
TRH Front Lawn 2b										1	1	0.4%	1
Total Adults	18	2	95	2	111	4	6	22	15	3	278	100%	
Total Locations Recorded	1	1	2	1	4	1	1	1	6	3			
FO (%)	7.1%	7.1%	14.3%	7.1%	28.6%	7.1%	7.1%	7.1%	42.9%	21.4%			

Table 6. Number of amphibian and reptile captures, by life stage, recorded by each survey method at Sagamore Hill.

	Spotted salamander	E. red-backed salamander	Spring peeper	Gray treefrog	Wood frog			Snapping turtle	Painted turtle	N. diamond-backed terrapin	Eastern box turtle	Eastern garter snake
	egg mass	adult	adult	adult	egg mass	larvae	adult	adult	adult	nest	adult	adult
Calling Survey			43									
Egg Mass Count	14				93							
Visual Encounter Survey	15	2	40			920	1	1	1	22	9	
Cover Board												
Turtle Trap Survey								1	1			
Minnow Trap Survey			8	2		1655						1
Incidental Encounter			4		3	1000	10	2	4		6	2
Total	29	2	95	2	96	3575	11	4	6	22	15	3

Table 7. Percentage of adults and adult equivalents (adults represented by turtle shells, nests, egg masses, and larva) recorded by each survey method at Sagamore Hill. Derived from Table 6.

	Spotted salamander	E. red-backed salamander	Spring peeper	Gray treefrog	Wood frog	Snapping turtle	Painted turtle	N. diamond-backed terrapin	Eastern box turtle	Eastern garter snake	Total Recorded	% of Total	Total Number of Species
Anuran Calling Survey			45%								43	15.5%	1
Egg Mass Count	50%				84%						102	36.7%	2
Visual Encounter Survey	50%	100%	42%		2%	25%	17%	100%	60%		86	30.9%	8
Cover Board											0	0.0%	0
Turtle Trap Survey						25%	17%				2	0.7%	2
Minnow Trap Survey			8%		2%					33%	11	4.0%	3
Incidental Encounter			4%	100%	13%	50%	67%		40%	67%	34	12.2%	7
Total	100%	100%	100%	100%	100%	100%	100%	100%	100%	100%	278	100.0%	10

23

Amphibian Calling Surveys

Spring peepers were recorded at Woodpile Pond on two of four occasions, with a maximum calling index of three. They were also recorded at heron pond, on one of four occasions, with a calling index of three (Table 8). However, two surveys in April were conducted in mid-afternoon, when detection probability of spring peepers is low (Paton et al. 2003), so the detection frequencies are likely underestimates.

Table 8. Maximum calling index (CI) and estimated number of calling males recorded during anuran calling surveys at Sagamore Hill in 2002.

Site (# of surveys)	Date	Start Time	Spring peeper	
			CI	Estimated number
Woodpile Pond (4)	04/15/02	14:50	0	0
	04/18/02	15:18	1	3
	05/15/02	20:05	3	20
	06/11/02	19:47	0	0
Heron Pond (4)	04/15/02	15:36	0	0
	04/18/02	14:42	0	0
	05/15/02	19:19	3	20
	06/11/02	19:18	0	0

Egg Mass Counts

Twenty three wood frog egg masses were counted at Heron Pond on 3/25/02 and 70 at Woodpile Pond on 3/26/02. On a second count on 4/12/02, 14 spotted salamander egg masses were counted in Woodpile Pond, but there was no standing water in Heron Pond and no egg mass count was conducted.

Visual Encounter Surveys

A total of eight species were recorded in visual encounter surveys, with six species in wetlands and four in uplands (Tables 9 and 10). Wood frog and eastern box turtles were recorded in both wetlands and uplands. Among wetlands, Woodpile Pond had the greatest number of species and individuals whereas none were recorded in Eel Creek (Table 9). Among upland areas, the greatest number of species (4) were recorded in West Slope/Punchbowl whereas the greatest number of individuals, represented by 22 diamond-backed terrapin nests, were recorded on Cold Spring Harbor Beach (Table 10). Of four field areas surveyed, only a single eastern box turtle was recorded in The Pasture. Based on visual encounter surveys, the most wide-spread species was eastern box turtle, recorded from seven of twelve survey areas. Wood frogs were recorded from two areas, and all other species were only recorded from a single area (Tables 9 and 10).

Coverboards

No amphibians or reptiles were recorded in the course of 448 coverboard checks between April 16 and August 16 2002.

Turtle Trapping Surveys
From the three sites trapped, we caught one snapping turtle and one painted turtle, both at Woodpile pond (Table 11).

Minnow Trapping Surveys
Minnow trap surveys detected spring peeper and wood frog at both Woodpile Pond and Heron Pond, and an eastern garter snake at Heron Pond (Table 12). Wood frog larvae were more abundant in Woodpile pond than in Heron Pond.

Incidental Encounters
Seven species were recorded as incidental encounters from 7 locations, 6 of which were standardized survey sites. Based on number of locations recorded, the most widespread species were eastern box turtle (6 locations total) and wood frog (3 locations). Of the seven species recorded, wood frogs had the greatest numbers recorded (10 adults, plus 3 egg masses and 1000 larvae), followed by eastern box turtle (6 adults) and spring peeper (4 adults) (Table 13).

Table 9. Number of captures and total number of species recorded (S) during wetland/pond visual encounter surveys at Sagamore Hill, 2002. The capture rate (in parentheses) is number of individuals divided by search hours.

Site	Habitat	Search Hours	Spotted salamander (egg masses)	Spring peeper	Wood frog (larvae)	Snapping turtle	Painted turtle	Eastern box turtle	S
					Species				
Eel Creek Salt Marsh	salt marsh	4.90							0
Heron Pond	vernal pond	0.87		4 (4.6)				1 (1.15)	2
Woodpile Pond	permanent pond	5.27	15 (2.85)	6 (1.14)	920 (175)	1 (0.19)	1 (0.19)		5
Wetlands total		11.04	15 (1.36)	10 (0.9)	920 (88.3)	1 (0.09)	1 (0.09)	1 (0.09)	6

26

Table 10. Number of captures and total number of species recorded (S) during upland visual encounter surveys at Sagamore Hill, 2002. The capture rate (in parentheses) is number of individuals divided by search hours.

			Species					
Site	Habitat	Search Hours	Eastern red-backed salamander	Wood frog	Eastern box turtle	Northern diamond-backed terrapin (nests)	Total Adults	S
CSH Beach	coastal beach	8.02				22 (2.74)	22 (2.74)	1
Cousin Beech Woods	deciduous forest	10.40			2 (0.19)		2 (0.19)	1
Heron Pond Woods	deciduous forest	8.30			2 (0.24)		2 (0.24)	1
Rifle Pit/South Slope	deciduous forest	8.92			2 (0.22)		2 (0.22)	1
WestSlope/Punchbowl	deciduous forest	8.78	2 (0.23)	1 (0.11)	1 (0.11)		4 (0.46)	3
	forest total	36.40	2 (0.05)	1 (0.03)	7 (0.19)		10 (0.27)	3
Old Barn	field	1.90						0
Old Orchard	field	3.75						0
The Field	field	3.67						0
The Pasture	field	3.92			1 (0.26)		1 (0.26)	1
	field total	13.23			1 (0.08)		1 (0.08)	1
	Uplands Total	57.65	2 (0.03)	1 (0.02)	8 (0.14)	22 (0.38)	33 (0.57)	4

27

Table 11. Number of turtle captures in turtle traps at Sagamore Hill, 2002. Capture rate (in parentheses) is number of captures per 100 trap nights.

							Species		
Site	Habitat	First Date	Last Date	#Nights	#Traps	Trap Nights	Snapping turtle	Painted turtle	
Heron Pond	vernal pond	4/15/2002	6/13/2002	9	5	45			
Woodpile Pond	permanent pond	4/16/2002	6/13/2002	8	2-5	31	1 (3.23)	1 (3.23)	
Eel Creek	salt marsh	5/13/2002	6/13/2002	5	5	30			

Table 12. Number of amphibian and reptile captures during minnow trap surveys at Sagamore Hill, 2002. Capture rate (in parentheses) is number of captures per 100 trap nights.

							Species		
Site	Habitat	First Date	Last Date	#Nights	#Traps	Trap Nights	spring peeper	wood frog (larvae)	Eastern garter snake
Heron Pond	vernal pond	4/15/2002	8/16/2002	12	4	48	7 (14.6)	2 (4.2)	1 (2.1)
Woodpile Pond	permanent pond	4/15/2002	8/16/2002	12	4	48	1 (2.1)	1653 (3444)	0

Table 13. Number of amphibians and reptiles recorded as incidental encounters at 7 locations at Sagamore Hill in 2002.

Location	Spring peeper	Gray treefrog	Wood frog			Snapping turtle	Painted turtle	Eastern box turtle	Eastern garter snake
	adult	adult	egg mass	larvae	adult	adult	adult	adult	adult
Heron Pond	1		3		9			3	
Woodpile Pond	3	2		1000		2	4		
The Field									1
The Pasture					1			1 plastron	
TRH Front Lawn 2b									1
Heron Pond Woods								1	
Cousin Beech Woods								1	
Total Captures	4	2	3	1000	10	2	4	6	2
Total # of localities	2	1	1	1	2	2	1	4	2

Discussion

Community Composition

Of the 38 species of amphibians and reptiles native to and resident on Long Island (Noble 1927) and 36 originally native to Nassau county (Schlauch 1978a), we recorded 10 in this inventory. This represents 91% (10/11) of the species known to have occurred historically at SAHI, 59% (10/17) of the species that may have occurred here, and 34% (10/29) of the local species pool (Table 1). The low species richness of amphibians and reptiles at SAHI is a reflection of several factors. Long Island is geologically young, formed of glacial moraine and outwash plains, and was only briefly connected to the continental mainland prior to sea level rise since the last glacial retreat (Pough and Pough 1968). Because of its recent creation, insular nature, and lack of certain habitats, Long Island lacks several species found on the adjacent mainland (Noble 1927). In addition, although SAHI occurs on Long Island's terminal moraine, where species richness on Long Island is greatest (Noble 1926), its small size (83 acres) and minimal freshwater habitat limit the number of species it can support. It has no freshwater stream or riparian habitat, and only two small freshwater ponds, one of which (Heron pond) appears to be a relatively short hydroperiod vernal pond. It is also likely that urbanization and other habitat changes have also reduced species richness at SAHI, but there is no historic record here to compare with.

In comparison, 22 species have been recorded at nearby Muttontown preserve (Lindberg 1994), which contains 500+ acres and a greater amount and variety of wetlands. This comparison, however, is a bit more complicated. The species list for Muttontown Preserve was accumulated over many years, whereas that reported here for SAHI is based on a single year. Moreover, 2002 was a dry year on Long Island, as shown by a lack of water in Heron Pond for much of the field season. Detecting amphibians and reptiles is more difficult in dry years, and some species actually present may have gone undetected. Thus, it is possible that over time, the documented species richness of SAHI may increase. However, even when these factors are considered, the fact remains that SAHI is limited in the number of species it is capable of supporting.

Although amphibians numerically dominated the herpetofauna recorded, accounting for 82% of individuals recorded, in terms of species richness the herpetofaunal community of SAHI is evenly divided between amphibians and reptiles, five species each. This is roughly proportionate to the structure of the local species pool, 16 amphibians and 13 reptiles (Table 1). However, SAHI community structure deviates from that of the local species pool in the relative contribution of snakes and turtles. Whereas the local species pool consisted of five turtle and eight snake species and SAHI potentially once supported four species of turtle and five species of snake (Table 1), SAHI now supports four turtle and only one snake species. This suggests that snake species richness may have declined on Cove Neck, perhaps due to urbanization and other habitat changes (Ziminski 1970, Kjoss and Litvaitis 2001).

Important Sites and Habitats

That the two wetland habitats, Woodpile pond and Heron pond had the greatest numbers of species recorded at them (Table 5) highlights the critical importance of wetlands to amphibians and reptiles. Yet, the majority of species recorded at SAHI are primarily terrestrial and spend most of the year in woodland and field habitats. For example, spotted salamander, spring peeper, wood frog, and gray treefrog only utilize wetlands for reproduction. They otherwise forage, hibernate, and spend most of their time in the uplands, primarily woodlands, up to several hundred meters from breeding ponds. These amphibians require both wetland and terrestrial habitats. In contrast, the red-backed salamander is terrestrial, and does not require wetland habitats. Box turtles are also terrestrial, largely a forest edge species that moves back and forth between forest and field habitats in response to seasonal temperature changes (Reagan 1974). Garter snakes utilize these two terrestrial habitats in much the same way. In addition, as evidenced in the data recorded at SAHI, both box turtles and garter snakes utilize wetlands as well, with both of these two species recorded at Heron pond. Wetlands provide food and a means of escaping extreme temperature in summer and thus are an important habitat feature for these two species as well.

Wetland habitats are the primary habitat for snapping and painted turtles. Yet, even these aquatic species are dependent on terrestrial habitats for nest sites. Both of these species, as well as box turtles, require open, well drained upland habitats such as fields for nesting. The diamondback terrapin, an estuarine species, is similar, differing only in that it utilizes the estuarine habitats of Eel creek and Cold Spring Harbor, and nests on the adjacent open beach.

Thus, in considering the habitats present at SAHI and the amphibian and reptile species that utilize them, it is important to recognize the dependence of most species on a combination of habitats. And, although a habitat or site in the park may only be briefly used by a species that brief use may be for a critical purpose, such as reproduction.

Stressors

Global stressors, which tend to affect large geographic areas, are often far removed from the ultimate cause or source whereas regional/local stressors work at a more localized level. Global stressors include ultraviolet-B radiation and atmospherically transported pollutants such as mercury and acid rain, and global warming (Blaustein et al. 1994; Blaustein and Dobson 2006). Stressors such as other heavy metals, chemicals found in fertilizers, herbicides, and pesticides, habitat degradation, disease such as viral and fungal infections, road mortality, and introduced species (Dunson et al. 1992; Blaustein 1994; Pechmann and Wilbur 1994; Daszak et al. 2000; Knapp and Matthews 2000) may also be widespread in their scope, but tend to be more variable across the landscape in their extent. Thus their impacts may be at either a regional or local level.

Few of these stressors are known to be operating at SAHI, although that may be because assessments have not yet been conducted. Pesticides such as arsenated lead was applied by spray to plantings during Theodore Roosevelt's lifetime (Bellavia and Curry 1995), but little is known about the amount, extent, or duration of these applications. Mercury is transported atmospherically and deposited, often far from the source, and can be accumulated by aquatic organisms to the point of causing lethal or sub-lethal effects. Mercury deposition occurs throughout the Northeast, and even aquatic systems of relatively undeveloped areas such as Acadia National Park (Bank et al. 2006) and Cape Cod National Seashore contain high levels of mercury. The problem occurs when low pH, in part due to acid rain, leads to elevated levels of mercury. This process has been linked to the decline of northern dusky salamanders at Acadia NP (Bank et al. 2006) and elevated, but non-lethal levels in snapping turtles (Golet and Haines 2001). Research elsewhere has shown that increased mercury levels increase abnormalities and mortality in larval southern leopard frogs (Unrine et al. 2004), a species that appears to be extirpated on Long Island (Feinberg, pers. comm.). Given that both acid precipitation and mercury deposition occur in the vicinity of SAHI (Kroenke et al. 2003; NYS DEC 2008) it is reasonable to conclude that SAHI is subjected to both of these stressors, but we are not aware of any data on mercury levels at SAHI.

As with mercury, low pH can increase the solubility of aluminum to levels toxic to amphibians (Clark and Hall 1985). Currently, freshwaters associated with SAHI are acidic. On five occasions between November 1999 and September 2000, pH of Woodpile Pond ranged from 5.25 to 6.82. At Heron pond, which only had water on 3/15/2000, pH was 5.49. Aluminum levels of samples collected on 3/26/01 ranged from 0.199 to 0.417 mg/L in Heron pond and from 0.022 to 0.041 mg/L in Woodpile Pond (Farris, unpublished data). These values are well within what is a very broad range for aluminum in Northeastern wetlands (Driscoll and Postek1996). Although data on the relationship between aluminum levels and amphibian impacts are limited and suggest inter-specific variation in aluminum tolerance, the aluminum levels and water pH at SAHI generally appear to be below documented LC50 (Lethal Concentration 50%) levels. However, the highest single sample value at SAHI (0.417 mg/L from a bottom sample of Heron pond) exceeded the lowest LC50 value for northern leopard frog (*Rana pipiens*) embryos, 0.403 mg/L at pH 4.8 (Linder and Grillitsch, 2000). This suggests that there may be some potential for aluminum impacts to amphibians at Heron pond, although its short hydro-period appears to be a more significant limiting factor.

Diseases are another group of potential stressors at SAHI. Three major diseases have been documented in Long Island amphibians (J. Feinberg, pers. comm.), although little is known of their population impacts, either directly or in combination with sub-lethal levels of contaminants. One disease implicated in global amphibian declines is Chytrid fungus, *Batrachochytridium dendrobatidis*. Although it appears to infect amphibians throughout most of the Northeast, there is no evidence of a significant impact in the region (Longcore et al. 2006). Less is known regarding diseases in reptiles. However, respiratory tract illnesses are present in Long Island box turtles (Lee 2004) and it could be introduced via the unauthorized release of animals "rescued" from harm's way. At present however, none of these diseases have been documented at or near SAHI

Lack of freshwater habitat can limit amphibians and reptiles in coastal areas, and SAHI does not have a great abundance of it, either historically or at present. Woodpile Pond and Heron Pond are the only freshwater ponds present, and a spring named "Frog Spring" by Roosevelt existed historically in what is now called "Cousin Beech Woods". Landscape alterations on private property north of Woodpile Pond have caused hydrological changes to a stream that once flowed east to Cold Spring Harbor (Bellavia and Curry 1995). Although its course is not well documented, the loss of this stream and other activities on this adjacent property appear to be related to the apparent loss of "Frog Spring".

Several more localized stressors have also been operating here, primarily in the form of habitat alterations at SAHI and on Cove Neck. Much of the original landscape was altered for agriculture and in the early 20th century there was much less woodland habitat at SAHI than there is now. Although good for woodland species, those that prefer open habitats or a mix, such as black racers, appear to be declining in some parts of New York State due to natural reforestation of fields (Gibbs et al. 2007) and loss of habitat to development. Maintenance of the cultural landscape at SAHI through field mowing is valuable for maintaining open habitat and habitat diversity, but can also be a stressor in that it exposes animals, especially turtles and snakes, to direct mortality if done during the warm months. The plans to restore more of the cultural landscape at SAHI by removing woody vegetation and maintaining these additional acres as open habitat (National Park Service 2007, 2008), have the potential to be beneficial, especially to reptiles, by enhancing basking and nesting habitat, but must be implemented carefully to minimize direct mortality, especially to New York State-listed Eastern Box Turtles.

The other significant local stressors at SAHI are those associated with urbanization. Urbanization reduces herpetofaunal diversity by extirpating some species, primarily those with complex life histories, specialized habitat requirements and/or large home ranges, and reducing the distribution of surviving species, mostly widespread generalists, to suitable habitat remnants (Schlauch 1976; Klemens 1985; Gibbs 1998; Germaine and Wakeling 2001; Rubbo and Kiesecker 2005). The extirpation and reduction of herpetofauna in urbanized landscapes is due to habitat loss, alteration, and fragmentation, pollution, and direct and indirect mortality. For example, in the Northeastern United States, populations of snapping turtle and box turtle are particularly vulnerable to extirpation from road kill (Gibbs and Shriver 2002). Another aspect of urbanization and fragmentation is the decreased ability of animals to move successfully between habitat patches, resulting in a lack of gene flow. Populations in isolated habitat patches, such as at SAHI or on Cove Neck in general, may be affected by decreased reproductive success, increased mortality, decreased genetic diversity, and are more vulnerable to extirpation (Primack 1993; Byers and Mitchell 2005). In addition, because of isolation, dispersal barriers, and lack of source populations, the odds of natural recolonization following a localized extinction are low (Scott et al. 2001).

Species at Risk, Urban Tolerance and Role of SAHI in Maintaining Local Herpetofauna

Most of the species recorded at SAHI in 2002 are fairly common, urban-tolerant species, which typically have small home ranges, simple life histories, and broad habitat tolerances (Schlauch 1976). Red-backed salamander, spring peeper, snapping turtle, painted turtle, and eastern garter snake are examples of urban tolerant species found at SAHI. However, a few of the species found at SAHI are locally uncommon species that generally do not persist well in urban-suburban landscapes. Most notable are wood frog, spotted salamander, gray treefrog, and box turtle. Schlauch (1978) recorded spotted salamanders in 1 of 18 "tracts", wood frog in 2 of 18, and gray treefrog in 2 of 18, and considered all three species to be extremely endangered in Nassau County. More recent data (Breisch and Ozard, in prep) confirm that these three species have very limited occurrence in Nassau County. Schlauch (1978) found box turtles to be more widespread, but still considered them endangered in the county. Complicating the assessment of status in box turtles is the fact that they typically live for several decades and individuals can persist long after a population is no longer viable. Despite being locally uncommon, these four species remain common at Muttontown preserve (Lindberg 1994) and they appear to still be somewhat common at SAHI as well.

Studies throughout the northeast U.S. indicate that both wood frog and spotted salamanders occur most frequently and in greater abundance in roadless, forested landscapes with relatively

34

long hydroperiod ponds (Baldwin and Vasconcelos 2003, Egan 2001, Egan and Paton 2004, Windmiller 1996). Their occurrence and abundance is negatively correlated with road density (Egan 2001), suggesting that their persistence in suburbanized landscapes will depend on remnants of relatively unfragmented forested landscapes. Moreover, since both of these species are primarily terrestrial, migrating annually to and from breeding ponds from up to a few hundred meters away (Windmiller 1996), viable populations require relatively intact woodland habitats extending this distance out from the breeding ponds. Based on the numbers of egg masses found at Woodpile and Heron Pond, SAHI, and Cove Neck appear to still provide a suitable landscape for wood frog. Its value to spotted salamanders may be less. There appear to be subtle differences between these two species in terms of optimum wetland characteristics, with wood frog abundance greatest in vernal ponds that dry out annually (Egan and Paton 2004), and spotted salamanders most abundant at "vernal" ponds that have semi-permanent to permanent hydroperiods (Windmiller 1996). These studies suggest that Heron Pond, with its short hydroperiod, is marginal at best for spotted salamanders. With only 15 egg masses found at Woodpile Pond, it does not appear that there is a very robust population of spotted salamanders at SAHI, though data collected in a wetter year might suggest otherwise.

The eastern box turtle is a *Special Concern* species in New York State (NYSDEC 2000). Box turtles have declined throughout much of their range due to habitat loss, fragmentation, suburbanization, over-collection, and road kill (Klemens 2000; Dodd 2001) and are declining on Long Island (Gibbs et al. 2007). Although they manage to survive in pockets of suitable habitat (Klemens 1993), even with seemingly intact habitat present, as in parks and nature preserves, populations may decline due to road-related mortality and collecting (Schlauch 1976). Box turtles are still considered common at Muttontown Preserve (Lindberg 1994) and the recording of 11 live individuals at SAHI (Table 14) during this survey suggests they may still be fairly common in and around SAHI.

Given what is now known about the movements of most species and the impacts of urbanization, it is clear that the persistence of many species in suburbanized landscapes will be limited to landscapes where patches of several hundred acres of reasonably intact native habitat are present. For some species, even this will not be adequate. Such patches will more than likely contain a park, preserve or similar "greenspace" at its "core", and it is in this capacity that SAHI is most important. Cove Neck provides a landscape of relatively low density suburban development with much of the native vegetation still intact and with SAHI as a core of protected habitat needed to support populations of box turtles and other native amphibians and reptiles in what is the least urbanized corner of Nassau County. Moreover, the above pertains to the estuarine habitats at SAHI as well. The Oyster Bay and Cold Spring Harbor system supports one of the larger populations of diamondback terrapins in New York (Morreale 1992) and though only a small portion of this system, SAHI contributes to it, primarily in terms of providing a nesting area.

Population Trends
Nassau County experienced tremendous urbanization in the latter half of the 20th century, primarily in the first half of that period. Of the 35 native species he analyzed (diamond-backed terrapin was excluded) Schlauch (1978) categorized seven species as extinct and 16 as extremely endangered. However, SAHI is located, is the least urbanized part of the county (Schlauch 1978a) and of the 18 equal-sized "tracts" created for the purpose of analyzing herpetofaunal

Table 14. Size, sex, and age of all turtles captured at Sagamore Hill in this survey. R and L refer to left and right respectively. CL=carapace length, CW=carapace width, PL=plastron length, PW=plastron width, Wt=weight.

Turtle Species	Location	Date	Scutes Notched	Turtle ID#	Method	Behavior	Sex	Age (years)	CL (mm)	CW (mm)	PL (mm)	PW (mm)	Wt (g)	Gravid
Snapping	Woodpile Pond	04/16/02	L11	7000	VES	under water	male	10-15	344.5	293.4	237.4	219.3	10400	no
Painted	Woodpile Pond	04/16/02	R1	1	VES	under water	female	10-15	150.5	110.0	147.5	100.2	0	no
Painted	Woodpile Pond	05/14/02	R2	2	Trap	in trap	male	10	142.0	103.0	130.9	84.6	320	no
Box	West Slope/Punch Bowl	04/15/02	R1	1	VES	basking	male	>16	154.4	129.4	0.0	85.3	525	no
Box	Heron Pond Woods	05/13/02	R2	2	VES	stationary	male	>22	155.5	117.4	130.3	86.1	565	no
Box	Heron Pond Woods	05/14/02	R1,2	3	IE	stationary	female	>20	136.0	105.4	136.5	178.2	530	no
Box	Cousin Beech Woods	06/10/02	R3	4	VES	stationary	male	>20	149.0	116.5	0.0	83.0	590	no
Box	Cousin Beech Woods	06/10/02	R1,3	5	VES	stationary	male	>20	169.5	128.2	0.0	88.4	665	no
Box	Heron Pond	06/11/02	R2,3	6	IE	basking	male	Adult	160.8	125.5	0.0	93.8	735	no
Box	Heron Pond	08/13/02	R2,3	6	VES	stationary	female	>16	130.5	103.3	130.6	85.5	450	no
Box	Rifle Pit/South Slope	09/09/02	R4	7	VES	stationary	male	>20	157.6	121.9	0.0	87.9	600	no
Box	Rifle Pit/South Slope	09/09/02	R1,4	8	VES	stationary	male	>20	160.5	129.6	0.0	102.7	690	no
Box	The Pasture	06/11/02	R9	20	VES	stationary	female	>18	142.7	112.2	0.0	84.6	595	yes
Box	Cousin Beech Woods	09/10/02	L1 R2	102	IE	stationary	male	>20	142.9	110.5	0.0	88.3	505	no

36

species status, the one in which SAHI is located was the most species rich, with 18 of 35 species recorded from 1960 to 1976 (Schlauch 1978a). More recent data collected in the 1990's show this to still be the case, with 21+ species recorded in the northeast corner of the county (Breisch and Ozard, in prep.). Although these recent data suggest that species loss in northeastern Nassau county has not been as severe as elsewhere in the county, there has, none the less, been a significant loss of herpetofauna in Nassau county. In recent "Herp Atlas" surveys (Breisch and Ozard, in prep.), 10 of the 35 species were not recorded at all and 11 others were recorded from 4 or fewer survey quadrangles.

While the herpetofauna of SAHI, particularly snakes, has likely declined due to urbanization impacts and possibly also from habitat change following the decline of agriculture on Cove Neck, without any historic data, it is impossible to determine trends for most of the species currently or formerly present here. The only exception to this is painted turtle, which has declined.

Management Recommendations
1. Monitor/Prevent/Mitigate External Threats. Considering that the herpetofauna of SAHI is largely affected by activities in the adjacent landscape, to the extent possible, the park needs to ensure that activities in the "neighborhood" are consistent with protection of native wildlife, including herpetofauna. Potential activities that could negatively affect amphibians and reptiles include applications of pesticides, anything that increases vehicular traffic, anything that pollutes or diminishes ground or surface waters, anything that increases the abundance of "subsidized predators" such as raccoons and feral cats.

2. Monitor/Prevent/Mitigate Internal Threats. Ensure the activities listed above do not take place on NPS property. In particular, ensure that runoff from park roads and parking lots is not contributing to pollution of groundwater and Woodpile pond.

3. Maintain Habitat Diversity. The amphibians and reptiles currently utilizing SAHI require a combination of woodland, field, and wetland habitat to provide for all aspects of their life cycles. Ensuring woodland health is important but concern for such health should recognize that natural woodlands contain dead and dying trees and an abundance of downed, rotting logs. Such dead snags and coarse woody debris are important habitat for many species of amphibians and reptiles, as well as cavity nesting birds and small mammals. In open habitats associated with the cultural core of the park, to the extent that it is possible, maintain as native grasses and forbs mowed infrequently, rather than "lawn".

4. Minimize Direct Mortality From Vehicles. Vehicular traffic and mowing activities, in particular, can cause direct mortality, particularly of snakes and turtles. Snakes often bask on roads in spring and autumn. Box turtles frequently cross roads and their populations are very sensitive to traffic impacts (Gibbs and Shriver 2002). Ensure that speed limits and speed bumps, if necessary, limit road kill and consider erecting "Turtle Crossing" signs on the park entrance road.

5. Minimize Direct Mortality From Mowing Operations. Box turtles and snakes typically use field habitats, and three species of turtles at SAHI (box, painted, snapping) use fields for nesting,

which generally occurs in late May through early July. Mowing should be conducted in a way that minimizes potential for direct mortality. There are a number of ways to do this, depending on how a particular area is being managed. For areas being maintained as lawn, it is best to mow frequently, so that the grass is close-cropped and turtles are readily observed by staff operating mowers and can be avoided. If grass has gotten taller, having a person walk ahead of the mower to check for turtles and chase away snakes is also useful.

Fields and pastures (as opposed to lawns) at SAHI are also maintained as part of the cultural landscape and their long term maintenance also benefits many species of wildlife dependant on edge or early successional stage habitat. This includes snakes and turtles, which use fields and their edges for basking and nesting. In particular, box turtles spend much of their time at the edge between fields and woodlands (Reagan 1974). Although maintaining fields at SAHI is beneficial in the long term for box turtles and other reptiles here, it must be done in a way that minimizes the risk of killing them with mower blades and/or tractor wheels. Ideally, fields should be mowed annually, during the cold months, because the box turtle activity season, on average, extends from 21 April until 24 October on western Long Island (Cook 1996). Thus, mowing fields from November until mid-April poses minimal risks to box turtles and other reptiles. The worst times of year to mow would be June-early July, which is generally when turtles nest, and in mid to late spring and late summer-early fall, when they often bask at field edges. If mowing must occur in summer, it should be done during the hottest months (July-August) to reduce the risk of mower/turtle encounters, but never following rain, which stimulates activity at this time of year. Turtles tend to avoid open areas during times of drought and high heat intensity, making the heat of day on hot dry, days the best time to mow, if necessary, during the active season.

Mowers with rotary blades or sickle bars are preferable to reel or flail mowers. Rotary blades and sickle bars are oriented horizontally and, if set to cut at least seven inches above ground, they will safely pass over many small animals and wear more slowly (MA NHESP 2007). Field mowing should always start in the center and spiral outward, so animals in the field are pushed out away from the mower.

Species Accounts

Spotted Salamander (*Ambystoma maculatum*)

The spotted salamander is widely distributed throughout the eastern United States and southeastern Canada (Petranka 1998) and in New England and New York it occurs both inland and along the coastal plain, down to sea level (Klemens 1993, Gibbs et al. 2007). They occur primarily in forested landscapes and breed in vernal and semi-permanent ponds (Petranka 1998). Outside of the breeding season, spotted salamanders are terrestrial, primarily subterranean, and many disperse as far as 200 to 400 meters from their breeding ponds (McDonough and Paton 2007). Ditmars (1905) noted its distribution in the vicinity of NYC was "sparing" and Sherwood (1895) considered them "not as common as marbled salamanders". However, Engelhardt (1914) considered them common on Long Island and Noble (1927) considered spotted salamanders to be widespread and common in the New York area. Considering what is now known of its local distribution, it would appear that Noble's assessment was correct.

Spotted salamanders are most abundant on unfragmented, roadless, forested landscapes with relatively large (>1000 square meter), deep (>1 m), fishless, permanent or semi-permanent ponds (Windmiller 1996, Egan and Paton 2004) and hence are not well adapted to persist in urbanized landscapes (Rubbo and Kiesecker 2005). However, they are able to persist in suburban and agricultural landscapse where forest cover exceeds ca. 30-50% (Homan et al. 2004, Gibbs et al. 2007). Spotted salamanders declined in Brooklyn and Queens as a result of urbanization (Schlauch 1976) and Schlauch (1978) considered them endangered in Nassau County. In more recent surveys, although more widespread in Suffolk County, spotted salamanders were reported from only three topo quads in Nassau County (Breisch and Ozard, in prep). Thus, the small population of spotted salamanders breeding in Woodpile Pond represents one of only a handful of known populations in Nassau County.

Eastern Red-backed Salamander (*Plethodon cinereus*)

The Eastern Red-backed salamander is a lungless, terrestrial salamander that is widespread and common throughout the Northeast, including New York State (Gibbs et al 2007) and New England (Klemens 1993). They occur as a number of different color morphs, with the red striped and or lead-backed (unstriped) the two most common and widespread (Petranka 1998). Although they reach their greatest density in well drained deciduous and mixed forests with well developed leaf litter (Gibbs et al. 2007) and in some forest ecosystems they dominate vertebrate biomass (Burton and Likens 1975), they are not necessarily restricted to mature forest habitats (Klemens 1993). At Cape Cod National Seashore, they can also be found in open habitat such as powerlines and under woody debris deposited by storm surge at the upper limits of salt marshes (R. Cook, pers. obs.). Because all embryonic and larval development takes place within the "aquatic" environment within the egg membrane, red-backed salamanders are completely terrestrial and do not require wetlands for reproduction. This attribute, in conjunction with their small home range and limited movements, has facilitated their widespread distribution and made them one of the most urban tolerant amphibians (Schlauch 1976), capable of persisting in small woodland patches in highly fragmented urban landscapes (Gibbs 1998).

Historically, red-backed salamanders were considered widespread and very common on Long Island (Noble 1927). There are many historic records from Long Island (Bishop 1941) and they are "found in woodlands everywhere" (Yeaton 1968). Although, their numbers have undoubtedly been reduced by urbanization, red-backed salamanders remain the most widespread and abundant salamander on Long Island and have recently been recorded widely from Nassau County (Breisch and Ozard, in prep.). Only two individuals were recorded at SAHI during this survey. This species is usually abundant where it occurs and readily found under logs and similar cover. However, most of the population is usually below the surface, and decreased soil moisture further reduces the numbers present on the surface (Petranka 1998). There was plenty of coarse woody debris to search under at SAHI and the low encounter rate observed here may reflect true rarity or simply the dry conditions present in 2002.

Gray Treefrog (*Hyla versicolor*)
The gray treefrog occurs throughout most of the eastern United States as a pair of sibling species distinguishable from each other in the field only by voice (Conant and Collins 1998). The species which occurs on Long Island, *Hyla versicolor*, is found throughout the Northeast and Canada (Klemens 1993). The gray treefrog has large toe pads, orange/yellow coloration on the underside of the hind limbs, and lives high in trees and shrubs, descending to wetlands to breed (Behler and King 1979). Their color ranges from gray to brown, green, light gray, to almost white depending on activity and environmental conditions (Conant and Collins 1998).

Historically, gray treefrogs were widespread and common on Long Island (Ditmars 1905; Noble 1927), with Overton (1914) stating its call was the most commonly heard and widely known frog call on Long Island. Gray treefrogs declined regionally in the latter half of the 20th century. By the 1930's Leng and Davis (1930) noted their increasing rarity on Staten Island, as did Mathewson (1955), although Kieran (1959) considered it common in NYC parks. In Connecticut, urbanization and pollution have extirpated or greatly reduced gray treefrogs (Klemens 1993). On Long Island, DDT spraying has also contributed to their decline (Schlauch and Burnley 1968) and Schlauch (1978) considered them extremely endangered in Nassau County. There are about 10 known populations of gray treefrogs at SAHI on western Long Island (west of Suffolk County) (Breisch and Ozard, in prep.) making the population at SAHI significant locally. However, its size is uncertain. Two individuals calling from Woodpile Pond were recorded incidentally on 6/11/2002. Because gray treefrogs have a relatively low detection probability (Weir et al. 2005) and only two nighttime calling surveys were conducted in May and June, when gray treefrogs call on Long Island (R. Cook, pers. obs.), it is possible that gray treefrogs are actually more abundant. More intensive calling surveys are needed to better determine their status at SAHI.

Spring Peeper (*Pseudacris crucifer*)
The spring peeper is widespread throughout the eastern United States and Canada (Klemens 1993) and ubiquitous, breeding in a wide range of wetland habitats. Its unique, high-pitched breeding call is often a deafening chorus of hundreds of individuals. These loud and distinct calls, in combination with a prolonged calling season that stretches from mid-March to mid-May (Overton 1914), make it one of the most readily detected of local anurans (cite someone here). Spring peepers are terrestrial outside of the breeding season, and utilize a broad range of terrestrial habitats (Gibbs et al. 2007). Historically, spring peepers were widespread and common in the New York Metropolitan-Long Island area (Ditmars 1905; Noble 1927; Yeaton 1968) and

because it is among the most urban tolerant of amphibians (Gibbs 1998), spring peepers still persist in many patches of remnant habitat on Long Island (Breisch and Ozard, in prep.).

The spring peeper was recorded from both Woodpile Pond and Heron Pond (with a calling index value of 3) and appears to be common at SAHI.

Wood Frog (*Rana sylvatica*)
The wood frog has an extensive range that includes Appalachia, the Northeast, most of Canada, and Alaska (Conant and Collins 1998). It is widespread in New England, occurring both inland and on the coastal plain (Klemens 1993) and has a similar distribution in New York State (Gibbs et al. 2007). Wood frogs are terrestrial, typically associated with forested landscapes, except during the breeding season when they breed in fishless vernal pools (Conant and Collins 1998). Breeding in early spring (late-February-March), the wood frog is an explosive breeder. Often a large percentage of a population migrates to ponds synchronously, laying eggs together in large floating masses. They breed in greatest abundance at vernal ponds with short to intermediate hydro-periods (Egan and Paton 2004) and equally use both closed and open canopy ponds (Skelly et al. 2002).

Historically, Noble (1927) considered wood frogs widespread and common although Ditmars (1905) considered them abundant but limited in occurrence. Wood frogs were widespread on Long Island with most records from the glacial moraines (Schlauch and Burnley 1968). Outside of the breeding season, wood frogs range far from their breeding ponds (Berven and Grudzien 1990). Consequently, wood frog abundance is now positively correlated with unfragmented and roadless forested landscapes with vernal ponds (Egan and Paton 2004) and wood frogs are not well adapted to urbanization (Klemens 1993; Gibbs 1998; Rubbo and Kiesecker 2005), particularly since vernal ponds are often filled in during urbanization (Campbell 1974). Latham (1971b) describes how a very large population of wood frogs, once so common on eastern Long Island that he made no effort to record them, declined dramatically after a wetland was drained after World War I. Thus, by the 1950's, wood frogs were limited to scattered patches of woodland habitat on western Long Island (Kieran 1959) and by the 1970's they had declined throughout much of Long Island (Schlauch 1978b). Current records are limited, but some populations still persist in Nassau and Suffolk Counties (Breisch and Ozard, in prep.).

Because each female lays one egg mass (Egan and Paton 2004), the 23 egg masses counted at Heron Pond on 3/25/02 and the 70 egg masses at Woodpile Pond on 3/26/02 represent 93 females. In comparison, at Cape Cod National Seashore, in annual monitoring at 12 vernal ponds in close proximity within a patch of unfragmented forest larger than SAHI, the total number of wood frog egg masses has exceeded 93 in only two of seven years (R. Cook, unpublished data). This suggests that SAHI supports a modest population of this locally uncommon species.

Snapping Turtle (*Chelydra serpentina*)
The snapping turtle occurs from southern Canada, south through the mid-west and east coast, down to Florida and the Gulf of Mexico (Ernst et al. 1994). It is abundant and widespread in New York State (Gibbs et al. 2007) and New England (Klemens 1993), and is the largest freshwater turtle in the northeastern United States. Although snapping turtles occur in nearly all freshwater habitats and also in brackish marshes, adults tend to occur more frequently in

permanent water bodies and are most abundant in shallow, muddy ones (Klemens 1993; Cook et al. 2007). Typical of all turtles, eggs are laid on land. Female snapping turtles must emerge from wetlands and travel overland in search of nesting areas, generally open, sandy, sparsely vegetated patches (Gibbs et al. 2007). They are often seen crossing roads in late spring-early summer. Females dig nests and deposit eggs in loose sand or soil, and the hatchlings emerge in the late summer or early fall (Ernst et al. 1994).

Historically, snapping turtles were considered widespread and common throughout the Long Island area (Engelhardt 1913; Murphy 1916; Noble 1927). Because urbanization has created additional permanent ponds in this region (Schlauch 1976) and snapping turtles are largely aquatic, primarily nocturnal, and relatively tolerant of water pollution and pesticides, they are able to survive urbanization (Klemens 1985) and are widespread in and around New York City (Kieran 1959) and Long Island (Breisch and Ozard in prep). The four records of snapping turtle in Woodpile Pond during this survey include two captures of one adult male, plus two additional observations of a single turtle where there is no way to know if it was the marked adult male. This suggests there is only one individual, or perhaps a very small population present in this relatively small pond.

Painted Turtle (*Chrysemys picta*)

The painted turtle is the only North American turtle that ranges across the continent, from southern Canada down through the Pacific northwest, midwest, and the northeast coast to Louisiana, Georgia, and the Carolinas (Ernst et al. 1994). There are four subspecies, with English names that describe each species distribution. In the Northeast, including the Long Island region, the Eastern painted turtle (*C. p. picta*) and the Midland painted turtle (*C. p. marginata*) intergrade, forming a hybrid swarm (Pough and Pough 1968). Whereas the eastern painted turtle has an unmarked yellow plastron and the seams of the central and lateral carapace scutes are aligned and the midland painted turtle has a variable dark marking on the plastron and alternating seams on the carapacial scutes (Ernst et al. 1994), Long Island painted turtles are intermediate in these characters and are highly variable both within and among populations (Pough and Pough 1968).

In addition to a wide geographic distribution, painted turtles are widespread ecologically, occurring in a broad range of freshwater habitats, including vernal ponds. However, they prefer permanent, shallow, standing or slow-moving water bodies with soft bottoms and an abundance of aquatic vegetation (Ernst et al. 1994; Cook et al. 2007; Gibbs et al. 2007). Because of their abundance and habit of basking on rocks, logs, and clumps of vegetation, painted turtles are the region's most familiar and conspicuous turtle (Klemens 1993). Painted turtles are highly aquatic, feeding and hibernating in ponds. However, they lay their eggs on land and, as with all aquatic turtles, must leave the relative safety of the wetland and travel overland to patches of open habitat with well drained soils to nest.

Historically, painted turtles were considered widespread and very abundant in the New York City-Long Island region (Engelhardt 1913; Murphy 1916; Noble 1927). Because permanent water bodies tend to survive urbanization and have increased in some instances through the damming of streams, painted turtles in the NYC-Long Island region survived 20th century urbanization (Mathewson 1955; Kieran 1959; Schlauch 1978b) and remain widespread today.

They occur in most any natural area on Long Island with a permanent pond or lake (Breisch and Ozard, in prep).

Theodore Roosevelt Jr. wrote of Woodpile Pond that "countless turtles sat on the rotten logs that lay there, or slowly swam over its surface, their heads sticking out of the green scum like small periscopes" (Bellavia and Curry 1995). This describes the basking habit of painted turtles and suggests they were once fairly numerous in Woodpile Pond. In this survey, there were a total of six painted turtle records. These included the capture of two adults, one of each sex (Table 14), plus two observations without capture that both involved two individuals. Although it is impossible to determine how many painted turtles were actually present in Woodpile Pond, these data suggest a fairly small population is present today and that the population of painted turtles here has declined since the historic period. Causes for the decline are uncertain. Although there is concern over impacts of contaminants from road and parking lot runoff into Woodpile Pond, painted turtles are well known for their ability to persist in polluted habitats (Klemens 1993). Roads and associated road kill can be a significant stressor on turtle populations (Gibbs and Shriver 2002), and considering the proximity of Woodpile Pond to roads and parking lots at SAHI, another possible cause of their decline here is direct mortality to nesting females and hatchlings attempting to head for the pond after emerging from the nest. Although we can't be certain of the causes, there is little doubt that painted turtles have declined at SAHI from common to uncommon.

Northern Diamond-backed Terrapin (*Malaclemys terrapin terrapin*)

The northern diamond-backed terrapin is a sub-species of the diamond-backed terrapin, a species that ranges along the coast from Texas to Cape Cod, Massachusetts. Northern diamond-backed terrapins range from Cape Hatteras, North Carolina to Cape Cod (Conant and Collins 1998). In New York, diamond-backed terrapins occur primarily along the coast of Long Island, both north and south shore (Morreale 1992). Terrapins are unique in that they are the only species of turtle restricted to estuaries (Morreale 1992) and they are typically found wherever extensive salt marsh habitat has developed, such as behind barrier beaches and within deep embayments. Although they spend most of their time in salt marshes, where they forage primarily on mollusks and crabs, female diamond-backed terrapins must emerge onto land to lay eggs, nesting in dunes, along roads and trails, and other open situations, often several hundred meters from water (Brennessel 2006). On western Long Island, terrapins nest from the first week of June through the third week of July (Cook 1989; Feinberg and Burke 2003).

Historically, diamond-backed terrapins were widespread and abundant on Long Island. However, they were highly valued as a delicacy (Smith 1899) and by the late 19th-early 20th century they had declined due to overharvesting (Engelhardt 1913; Murphy 1916). Terrapins remained rare to uncommon in the region during the first half of the 20th century, but appeared to be rebounding by the second half (Yeaton 1972; Morreale 1992). By the late 20th century, diamond-backed terrapins had recovered in many areas, including Long Island, although it was noted that the continuation of this recovery was threatened by renewed loss of habitat, commercial take, drowning in crab pots, and roadkill (Cook 1989; Wood and Herlands 1997). Recent data indicate that terrapins are widespread on the Long Island coast (Breisch and Ozard, in prep).

43

In this survey, a total of 22 diamond-backed terrapin nests were recorded at SAHI, on the beach adjacent to Cold Spring Harbor (Table 5, 6, 10). Five were the remains of old nests (i.e. laid prior to 2002) and 17 were recently laid and predated, most likely by raccoons. Where raccoons are present, particularly as subsidized predators in urban-suburban areas, nest predation can be a significant problem. For example, at Jamaica Bay Wildlife Refuge on western Long Island, where there was a large increase in the raccoon population at the end of the 20th century, nest depredation by raccoons went from none in the early 1980's (Cook 1989) to 92.2% by the late 1990's (Feinberg and Burke 2003). Such high predation rates exceed those found in non-urban areas where populations of subsidized predators are not so high and threaten population viability (Ner and Burke 2008). Determining the extent of raccoon predation on the terrapins nesting on the beach at SAHI will require more intense monitoring than possible in this survey, but our observations suggest that predation rates here may also be excessive.

The Oyster Bay – Cold Spring Harbor system supports one of the larger populations of diamond-backed terrapins in New York State. Morreale (1992) captured 112 individuals in Mill Neck Creek (ca. 6 km west of SAHI) and observed terrapins there "in numbers too large to count". There are no data on total numbers of terrapins spread out across this entire system, nor do we know all of the nesting sites and their relative importance. Therefore, all we can really say is that SAHI appears to provide nesting habitat for modest numbers of diamond-backed terrapins within this system, and that the beach and salt marshes at SAHI should be viewed as a modest part of this larger habitat complex.

Eastern Box Turtle (*Terrapene carolina carolina*)

Eastern box turtles occur from Georgia and northern Alabama and Mississippi northward into southern Illinois and eastward (Conant and Collins 1998). In the northeast, box turtles are largely restricted to the coastal plain and major river valleys and extend northward into southern New England and up to Albany, NY (Klemens 1993). The eastern box turtle is a terrestrial species that typically occurs in areas that are a mix of woodland and open habitat. The habitat diversity provides the ability to shift habitats seasonally in response to changes in temperature and humidity (Reagan 1974), and, as with all turtles, well drained open habitats are needed for nesting. Eastern box turtles are frequently found foraging following spring and summer rains, and they will feed on slugs, fruits, vegetation, and carrion.

Historically, box turtles were widespread in the New York metropolitan area and considered abundant on Long Island (Smith 1899; Engelhardt 1913; Murphy 1916; Noble 1927). However, as urbanization progressed they began to decline. Citing automobiles as a cause, Kieran (1959) noted the decline of box turtles on western Long Island. The terrestrial nature of box turtles results in their being more widely dispersed across the landscape than aquatic amphibians and reptiles. Box turtles often engage in seasonal movements for nesting, hibernation, or feeding, and some individuals are transients that do not establish home ranges (Dodd 2001). All this movement across the landscape places box turtles at relatively greater risk of becoming road kill (Gibbs and Shriver 2002) or being collected for a pet in urban areas (Schlauch 1976), which, in conjunction with their late maturity and low rate of reproduction, make their populations unable to sustain the heavy adult mortality that typically occurs in urban areas. Thus, box turtle populations do not fare well on landscapes found in urban/suburban areas (Mitchell and

Klemens 2000) and have declined throughout much of their range due to habitat loss, fragmentation, over-collection, and road kill (Klemens 2000; Dodd 2001).

Box turtles are a species of *Special Concern* in New York State and have declined on Long Island (Gibbs et al. 2007). Schlauch (1978a) considered them endangered in Nassau County. Although there are still many widespread records from Long Island (Breisch and Ozard, in prep), individual box turtles are able to survive in pockets of suitable habitat, primarily in parks and habitat remnants (Klemens 1993). Moreover, box turtles are frequently moved around and released by people, and because they are very long lived, sometimes exceeding 100 years (Behler 2003), many of these recent records, especially on western Long Island, may not represent a viable population.

There were 11 individual box turtles, all adult, encountered in this survey, eight males and three females, one of which was gravid (Table 14). Another one of the females, #6 was the smallest box turtle recorded in this survey (carapace length 130.5 mm) and appears to be a young adult (Table 14). This suggests there is a small breeding population in and around SAHI and some recruitment is taking place, but we are unable to evaluate population viability. Given their patterns of movement (Dodd 2001) it is very likely that box turtles found at SAHI move across the landscape of Cove Neck, but we have no data on how far these individuals range beyond the boundaries of SAHI. Similarly, box turtles found at SAHI are undoubtedly part of a larger population present throughout Cove Neck, yet we have no data on the size of this population. All we know is that SAHI supports modest numbers of box turtles and may serve as a core reserve for box turtles inhabiting the Cove Neck Peninsula.

Although box turtles have quietly persisted at SAHI up to now, their future persistence here may require a more conscious effort. As detailed above in the Recommendations #4 and #5, road kill and mowing operations can cause significant mortality to box turtles and threaten their population viability. Considering the increased levels of vegetation management that will be necessary to maintain SAHI's cultural landscape in accordance with the recent General Management Plan (National Park Service 2007, 2008) it will be important to follows these recommendations.

Northern Ring-necked Snake (*Diadophis punctuatus edwardsii*)

As a species, the ring-necked snake ranges throughout the northeast United States and southern Canada southward through the mid-west and south-central states and northward along the Pacific coast (Ernst and Ernst 2003). The northern sub-species occupies the northeastern and Appalachian Mountain portion of that range (Conant and Collins 1998), is widespread in New York State, and often abundant as well (Gibbs et al. 2007). The northern ring-necked snake is a small, inconspicuous, primarily nocturnal species, typically found in moist woodlands with abundant cover where it feeds on small salamanders, especially red-backed salamanders and worms (Conant and Collins 1998; Ernst and Ernst 2003).

Historic accounts suggest that the ring-necked snake was not encountered very often in the New York City and Long Island area. Ditmars (1896) considered it somewhat rare and Noble (1927) considered it widespread, but desired habitat records. Engelhardt et al. (1915) noted only two locations, one of which was Port Jefferson, on Long Island's North Shore ca. 40 km east of

SAHI. Yeaton (1938) considered it probably the rarest snake on Long Island and Latham (1971a) considered it generally distributed on the east end of Long Island, but very secretive. Although "Historic" assessments of a species' abundance and/or distribution can sometimes turn out to be incorrect, especially for inconspicuous or "retiring" species, data collected through the late 1960's (including those of Latham) show that although ring-necked snakes occur the entire length of Long Island, on both the moraines and outwash plains (Schlauch 1974), they do not appear to be very common in occurrence or abundance.

Burnley (1968) observed a DOR adult ring-necked snake "at Cove Neck near Sagamore Hill" on July 3, 1963 and this species has more recently been recorded from two topo quads in northern Nassau County, Hicksville and Sea Cliff (Breisch and Ozard, in prep). However, there have been no other records of this species at SAHI, and none were observed during this survey. At Cape Cod National Seashore, ring-necked snakes represented 74% of all snake captures under coverboards during a three year period, with a capture rate of 0.0121 captures/board check (81 captures/6674 board checks)(R. Cook, unpublished data). During this survey at SAHI, coverboards identical to those used at Cape Cod and deployed in the same fashion were checked 448 times without producing any ring-necked snakes. Had the capture rate at SAHI equaled that of Cape Cod, the sampling effort at SAHI would have lead to 5.42 captures. Given these efforts, plus 36.4 search hours in woodland habitat with extensive searching under coarse woody debris, there does not appear to be a lack of sampling effort. However, considering the conditions in 2002, it is impossible to know if the ring-necked snake at SAHI is extirpated, rare, and/or had retreated below the surface in response to a lack of rain.

Eastern Garter Snake (*Thamnophis sirtalis sirtalis*)

The eastern garter snake is a sub-species of the common garter snake, which ranges throughout the United States, except for Texas and the southwest, and all of southern Canada (Ernst and Ernst 2003). The eastern garter snake occurs primarily east of the Mississippi River from Florida northward into New York and southern New England into Canada (Conant and Collins 1998). In New York and southern New England, garter snakes are widespread and common, both inland and along the coast, and are the most conspicuous and well known snake in this area (Klemens 1993; Gibbs et al. 2007). Garter snakes are found in a variety of habitats including meadows, marshes, woodlands, and cultivated and developed areas (Behler and King 1979). Historically they were considered the most common and widespread snake around New York City (Ditmars 1896) and Long Island (Engelhardt 1913). Although garter snakes are relatively urban tolerant because of their generalized habits (Schlauch 1976), as urbanization continued into the late 20th century, they have become less common and widespread (Ziminski 1970) and locally endangered in Nassau County (Schlauch 1978a) However, data from the New York State Herp Atlas (Breisch and Ozard, in prep), show they still remain the most common and widespread local snake.

Two adult eastern garter snakes were captured during this survey (one at Heron Pond on 4/17/02 and one on the Tennis Court Trail on 8/13/02), plus there was one observation without capture of an unknown individual on the edge of "The Field" on 9/9/02. These observations suggest they are uncommon but widespread at SAHI, both geographically and in terms of habitats used. Considering the amount of time and sampling effort at SAHI in 2002 (68.7 search hours and 448 coverboard checks) a total of three garter snake encounters seems relatively low. In the same year, at the William Floyd Estate in Mastic, Long Island, we had 17 garter snake encounters in the course of roughly twice as much sampling effort (126.5 search hours and 704 coverboard checks). Also in 2002, at three sites on western Long Island within the Jamaica Bay unit of Gateway NRA, we had 95 garter snake encounters in the course of roughly nine times the sampling effort (608 search hours and 3910 coverboard checks) (Cook, unpublished data).

Although these comparisons suggest that garter snakes are not very common at SAHI, the only historic "data" available are very general statements that garter snakes were common regionally (Ditmars 1896, Engelhardt 1913). Given how common garter snakes once were on Long Island, it is probable that their current scarcity at SAHI represents a decline, but in the absence of more specific historic data it is impossible to be certain.

Literature Cited

Baldwin, R. F. and D. Vasconcelos 2003. Ambystoma maculatum (Spotted Salamander) and Rana Sylvatica (Wood Frog) Habitat. Herpetological Review 34(4):353-354.

Bank, M. S., J. B. Crocker, S. Davis, D. K. Brotherton, R. Cook, J. Behler, and B. Connery. 2006. Population decline of northern dusky salamanders at Acadia National Park, Maine. Biological Conservation 130:230-238.

Behler, J. L. 2003. A 100-year-old Turtle. Curator's Report, Spring 2003. Wildlife Conservation Society, Bronx, New York.

Behler, J. L. and F. W. King. 1979. The Audubon Society Field Guide to North American Reptiles and Amphibians. Alfred A. Knopf, New York.

Bellavia, R. M. and G. W. Curry. 1995. Cultural landscape report for Sagamore Hill National Historic Site. USDI, National Park Service, Olmstead Center for Landscape Preservation.

Berven, K. A., and T. A. Grudzien. 1990. Dispersal in the wood frog (*Rana sylvatica*): implications for genetic population structure. Evolution 44:2047-2056.

Blaustein, A. R. 1994. Chicken little or Nero's fiddle? A perspective on declining amphibian populations. Herpetologica 50:85-97.

Blaustein, A. R., and A. Dobson. 2006. A message from the frogs. Nature 439:143-144.

Blaustein, A. R., P. D. Hoffman, D. G. Hokit, J. M. Kiesecker, S. C. Walls, and J. B. Hays. 1994. UV repair and resistance to solar UV-B in amphibian eggs: a link to population declines? Proceedings of the National Academy of Sciences 91:1791-1795.

Bishop, S. C. 1941. Salamanders of New York. Bulletin New York State Museum 324:1-365.

Breisch, A. R. and J. W. Ozard. in prep. The New York State Amphibian and Reptile Atlas 1990-1999. New York State Department of Environmental Conservation.

Brennessel, B. 2006. Diamonds in the marsh: a natural history of the diamondback terrapin. University Press of New England. Lebanon, New Hampshire.

Burnley, J. M. 1968. Some herpetological records from Nassau County, Long Island. Bulletin of the Maryland Herpetological Society 4 (2):52-54.

Burton, T. M. and G. E. Likens. 1975. Salamander populations and biomass in the Hubbard Brook Experimental Forest, New Hampshire. Copeia 1975:541-546.

Bury, R. B., and M. G. Raphael. 1983. Inventory methods for amphibians and reptiles. *In* J. F. Bell and T. Atterbury (eds.), Renewable Resources Inventories for Monitoring Changes and Trends, pp. 416-419. Oregon State University, Corvallis, Oregon.

Byers, D. L. and J. C. Mitchell. 2005. Sprawl and species with limited dispersal abilities. *In* E. A. Johnson and M. W. Klemens (eds.), Nature in Fragments: The Legacy of Sprawl, pp. 157-180. Columbia University Press, New York, New York.

Cagle, F. R. 1939. A system of marking turtles for future identification. Copeia 1939:170-173.

Campbell, C. A. 1974. Survival of amphibians and reptiles in urban environments. *In* J. H. Noyes and D. R. Progulske (eds.), A Symposium on Wildlife in an Urbanizing Environment, pp. 61-66. Planning and Resource Development Series No. 28, Holdsworth Natural Resource Center, University of Massachusetts, Amherst.

Clark, K. L. and R. J. Hall. 1985. Effects of elevated hydrogen ion and aluminum concentrations on the survival of amphibians embryos and larvae. Canadian Journal of Zoology 63:116-123.

Conant, R. and J. T. Collins. 1998. A Field Guide to Reptile and Amphibians: Eastern and Central North America. 3rd Edition Expanded. Boston:Houghton Mifflin Co.

Congdon, J. D., G. L. Breitenbach, R. C. van Loben Sels, and D. W. Tinkle. 1987. Reproduction and nesting ecology of snapping turtles (*Chelydra serpentina*) in southeastern Michigan. Herpetologica 43:39-54.

Congdon, J. D., S. W. Gotte, and R. W. McDiarmid. 1992. Ontogenetic changes in habitat use by juvenile turtles, *Chelydra serpentina* and *Chrysemys picta*. Canadian Field Naturalist 106:241-248.

Cook, B. 1989. A natural history of the diamondback terrapin. Underwater Naturalist 18:25-31.

Cook, R. P. 1978. Effects of acid precipitation on embryonic mortality of spotted salamanders (*Ambystoma maculatum*) and Jefferson salamanders (*Ambystoma jeffersonianum*) in the Connecticut Valley of Massachusetts. M.S. Thesis, University of Massachusetts, Amherst.

Cook, R. P. 1996. Movement and ecology of eastern box and painted turtles repatriated to human-created habitat. Ph.D. dissertation., City University of New York.

Cook, R. P. and C. A. Pinnock. 1987. Recreating a herpetofaunal community at Gateway National Recreation Area. pp. 151-154 *In* L. W. Adams and D. L. Leedy (eds.) Integrating man and nature in the urban environment. National Institute for Urban Wildlife, Columbia, Maryland.

Cook, R. P. and K. M. Boland. 2005. A comparison of approaches to counting egg masses of spotted salamander (*Ambystoma maculatum*). Herpetological Review (36):272-274.

Cook, R. P., K. M. Boland, S. J. Kot, J. Borgmeyer, and M. Schult. 2007. Inventory of aquatic turtles at Cape Cod National Seashore with recommendations for long term monitoring. Technical Report NPS/NER/NRTR-2007/091. National Park Service, Boston, Massachusetts.

Crother, B. I. (ED.). 2000. Scientific and Standard English Names of Amphibians and Reptiles of North America North of Mexico, with Comments Regarding Confidence in Our Understanding. Committee on Standard English and Scientific Names. Society for the Study of Amphibians and Reptiles Herpetological Circular No. 29.

Crother, B. I., J. Boundy, J. A. Campbell, K. De Quieroz, D. Frost, D. M. Green, R. Highton, J. B. Iverson, R. W. McDiarmid, P. A. Meylan, T. W. Reeder, M. E. Seidel, J. W. Sites Jr., S. G. Tilley, and D. B. Wake. 2003. Scientific and Standard English Names of Amphibians and Reptiles of North America North of Mexico: Update. Herpetological Review 34:196–203.

Crouch, W. B. and P. W. C. Paton. 2000. Using egg mass counts to monitor wood frog populations. Wildlife Society Bulletin 28:895-901.

Crouch, W. B. and P. W. C. Paton. 2002. Assessing the use of call surveys to monitor breeding anurans in Rhode Island. Journal of Herpetology 36:185-192.

Crump, M. L. and N. J.Scott.1994. Visual Encounter Surveys. *In* Heyer, R. W., M. A. Donnelly, R. W. McDiarmid, L. C. Hayek, M. S. Foster. 1994. Measuring and Monitoring Biological Diversity – Standard Methods for Amphibians. Pp 84-92. Smithsonian Institution Press. Washington, DC.

Daszak, P., L. Berger, A. A. Cunningham, A. D. Hyatt, D. E. Green, and R. Speare. 2000. Emerging Infectious Diseases and Amphibian Population Declines. Center for Disease Control. Vol. 5, No. 6.

Ditmars, R. L. 1896. The snakes found within fifty miles of New York City. Abstract of Proceedings of the Linnaean Society of New York 8:9-24.

Ditmars, R. L. 1905. The batrachians of the vicinity of New York City. Guide Leaflet Series No. 20, American Museum of Natural History. New York, New York.

Dodd, C. K. 2001. North American Box Turtles: A Natural History. Norman, University of Oklahoma Press.

Driscoll, C. T. and K. M. Postek. The chemistry of aluminum in surface waters. *In* G. Sposito, ed., The environmental chemistry of aluminum, pp. 363-418. CRC Press, Boca Raton, Florida.

Dunson, W. A., R. L. Wyman, and E. S. Corbett. 1992. A symposium on amphibian declines and habitat acidification. Journal of Herpetology 26:349-352.

Egan, R. S. 2001. Within-pond and landscape-level factors influencing the breeding effort of *Rana sylvatica* and *Ambystoma maculatum*. M.S. Thesis, University of Rhode Island, Kingston.

Egan, R. S., and P.W. Paton. 2004. Within-pond parameters affecting oviposition by wood frogs and spotted salamanders.Wetlands 24: 1-13.

Engelhardt, G. P. 1913. The reptiles of Long Island. Museum News 8:128-129.

Engelhardt, G.P. 1914. Amblystoma of Long Island. Copeia 8:2-4.

Engelhardt, G. P., J. T. Nichols, R. Latham, and R. C. Murphy. 1915. Long Island Snakes. Copeia 17:1-4.

Ernst, C. H., J. E. Lovich, and R. W. Barbour. 1994. Turtles of the United States and Canada. Smithsonian Institution Press, Washington D. C.

Ernst, C. H. and E. M. Ernst. 2003. Snakes of the United States and Canada. Smithsonian Institution Press, Washington D. C.

Feinburg, J. A., and R. L. Burke. 2003. Nesting ecology and predation of diamondback terrapins, *Malaclemys terrapin*, at Gateway National Recreation Area, New York. Journal of Herpetology 37: 517-526.

Germaine, S. S., and B. F. Wakeling. 2001. Lizard species distributions and habitat occupation along an urban gradient in Tucson, Arizona, USA. Biological Conservation 97:229-237.

Gibbs, J.P., 1998. Distribution of woodland amphibians along a forest fragmentation corridor. Landscape Ecology 13: 263-268.

Gibbs, J. P., and W. G. Shriver. 2002. Estimating the effects of road mortality on turtle populations. Conservation Biology 16:1647-1652.

Gibbs, J. P., A. R. Breisch, P. K. Ducey, G. Johnson, J. L Behler, and R. C. Bothner. 2007. The amphibians and reptiles of New York State. Oxford University Press, New York.

Golet, W. J. and T .A. Haines. 2001. Snapping turtles (*Chelydra serpentina*) as monitors for mercury contamination of aquatic environments. Environmental Monitoring and Assessment 71:211-220.

Grant, B. W., A. D. Tucker, J. E. Lovich, A. M. Mills, P. M. Dixon and J. W. Gibbons. 1992. The use of coverboards in estimating patterns of reptile and amphibian biodiversity. *In* D. R. McCullough and R. H. Barrett (eds.). Wildlife 2002: Populations, pp. 379-403. Elsevier Science Publication, Inc. London, England.

Harless, M., and H. Morlock. 1989. Turtles: Perspectives and Research. Robert E. Krieger Publishing Company, Inc. Malabar, Florida.

Heyer, R. W., M. A. Donnelly, R. W. McDiarmid, L. C. Hayek, M. S. Foster. 1994. Measuring and Monitoring Biological Diversity – Standard Methods for Amphibians. Smithsonian Institution Press, Washington D.C.

Homan, R. N., B. S. Windmiller, and J. M. Reed. Critical thresholds associated with habitat loss for two vernal pool-breeding amphibians. Ecological Applications 14:1547-1553.

Kieran, J. 1959. Natural History of New York City. Houghton-Mifflin Co. Boston, Massachusetts.

Kjoss, V. A. and J. A. Litvaitis. 2001. Community structure of snakes in a human-dominated landscape. Biological Conservation 98:285-292.

Klemens, M. W. 1985. Survivors in megalopolis: Reptiles of the urban Northeast. Discovery 18:22-25

Klemens, M. W. 1993. Amphibians and reptiles of Connecticut and adjacent regions. State Geological and Natural History Survey of Connecticut, Bulletin 112.

Klemens, M. W., editor. 2000. Turtle Conservation. Smithsonian Institution Press, Washington D. C.

Knapp, R. A., and K. R. Matthews. 2000. Non-native fish introductions and the decline of the Mountain Yellow-legged Frog from within protected areas. Conservation Biology 14:428-438.

Kroenke, A. E., E. L. Shuster, R. F .Bopp, and M .D. Gastrich. 2003. Assessment of historical and current trends in mercury deposition to New Jersey aquatic systems through analysis of sediment/soil cores. Research Summary. New Jersey Department of Environmental Protection, Division of Science, Research, and Technology. Trenton, New Jersey.

Latham, R. 1971a. Records of the ringneck snake on eastern Long Island. Engelhardtia 4:46.

Latham, R. 1971b. The wood frog on eastern Long Island. Engelhardtia 4:50.

Lee, S. M. 2004. Repatriation and health assessment of eastern box turtles (*Terrapene c. carolina*) at Caumsett State park, New York. M. S. Thesis, Hofstra University.

Leng, C.W. and W.T. Davis. 1930. Staten Island and its people: A history. 1609-1929. Lewis Historical Publishing Company, New York.

Lindberg, A. 1994. Amphibians and Reptiles of Muttontown Preserve. Nassau County Department of Recreation and Parks.

Linder, G. and B. Grillitsch. 2000. Ecotoxicology of metals. *In* D. W. Sparling, G. Linder, and C. A. Bishop (eds.), Ecotoxicology of amphibians and reptiles, pp. 325-459. SETAC Press, Pensacola, Florida.

Longcore, J. R, J. E. Longcore, A. P. Pessier, and W. A. Halteman. 2006. Chytridiomycosis widespread in anurans of northeastern United States. Journal of Wildlife Management 71:435-444.

Massachusetts Natural Heritage and Endangered Species Program. 2007. Draft mowing advisory guidelines in turtle habitat: pastures, successional fields, and hayfields. http://www.mass.gov/dfwele/dfw/nhesp/conservation/pdf/mowing_guidelines.pdf

Mathewson, R. F. 1955. Reptiles and amphibians of Staten Island. Proc. Staten Island Institute of Arts and Sciences Vol. XVIII: No.2.

McDonough, C. and P.W.C. Paton. 2007. Salamander dispersal across a forested landscape fragmented by a golf course. Journal of Wildlife Management 71:1163-1169.

Mitchell, J. C., and M. W. Klemens. 2000. Primary and secondary effects of habitat alteration. In: Turtle Conservation, p. 5-32. Klemens, M. W., Ed, Smithsonian Institution Press. Washington, DC.

Morreale, S. J. 1992. The status and population ecology of the diamondback terrapin, *Malaclemys terrapin*, in New York. Okeanos Ocean Research Foundation, Hampton Bays, New York.

Murphy, R. C. 1916. Long Island Turtles. Copeia 33:56-60.

National Park Service. 2007. Sagamore Hill National Historic Site, Final General Management Plan, Final Environmental Impact Statement. USDI, National Park Service, Northeast Region, Boston, Massachusetts.

National Park Service. 2008. Sagamore Hill National Historic Site, General Management Plan,USDI, National Park Service, Northeast Region, Boston, Massachusetts.

New York State Department of Environmental Conservation. 2000. Endangered Species Program. http://www.dec.state.ny.us/website/dfwmr/wildlife/endspec/

New York State Department of Environmental Conservation. 2008. Hydrogen ion concentration as pH (2006). Acid Deposition Monitoring Program. http://www.dec.ny.gov/chemical/38884.html

Ner, S. E. and R. L. Burke. 2008. Direct and indirect effects of urbanization on diamond-backed terrapins of the Hudson river bight:distribution and predation in a human-modified estuary. *In* Mitchell J. C. and R.E. Jung (eds.), Urban Herpetology. pp 107-117. Herpetological Conservation Vol. 3. Society for the Study of Amphibians and Reptiles. Salt Lake City, Utah.

Noble, G. K. 1926. The Long Island newt: a contribution to the life history of *Triturus viridescens*. American Museum Novitates 228:l-11.

Noble, G. K. 1927. Distributional list of the reptiles and amphibians of the New York City region. Guide Leaflet Series No.69, American Museum of Natural History, New York.

Overton, F. 1914. Long Island flora and fauna III: the frogs and toads (Order Salientia). Museum of the Brooklyn Institute of Arts and Science, Science Bulletin 2(3):21-40.

Paton, P. W. C., B. C. Timm, and T. Tupper. 2003. Monitoring pond-breeding amphibians: a protocol for the long-term coastal monitoring protocol at Cape Cod National Seashore. National Park Service, Wellfleet, Massachusetts.

Pechmann, J. H. K., and H. W. Wilbur. 1994. Putting declining amphibian populations in perspective: natural fluctuations and human impacts. Herpetologica 50:65-84.

Petranka, J. W. 1998. Salamanders of the United States and Canada. Smithsonian Institution Press, Washington, D. C.

Pough, F. H., and M. B. Pough. 1968. The systematic status of painted turtles (*Chrysemys*) in the northeastern United States. Copeia 1968:612-618.

Primack, R. B. 1993. Essentials of Conservation Biology. Sinauer Associates, Inc., Sunderland, Massachusetts.

Reagan D. P. 1974. Habitat selection in the three-toed box turtle, *Terrapene carolina triunguis*. Copeia 1974: 512-527.

Redmer, M. and S. E. Trauth. 2005.Wood Frog. *In* M. Lanoo (ed), Amphibian declines: the conservation status of United States species. pp 590-593. University of California Press, Berkeley.

Rubbo, M. J., and J. M. Kiesecker. 2005. Amphibian breeding distribution in an urbanized landscape. Conservation Biology 19: 504-511.

Schlauch, F. C. 1974. The biogeography of the herpetofauna of Long Island, NY. Unpubl. Ms.

Schlauch, F.C . 1976. City snakes, suburban salamanders. Natural History 85:46-53.

Schlauch, F. C. 1978a. New methodologies for measuring species status and their application to the herpetofauna of a suburban region. Engelhardtia 6: 30-41.

Schlauch, F. C. 1978b. Urban geographical ecology of the amphibians and reptiles of Long Island. In C.M. Kirkpatrick (ed.), Wildlife and People, pp. 25-41. John S. Wright Forestry Conference Proceedings, Cooperative Extension Service, Purdue University, West Lafayette, Indiana.

Schlauch, F. C. and Burnley, J. M. 1968. An annotated list of the salientians of Suffolk County, Long Island, New York. Bulletin Maryland Herpetological Society 4(4):74-75.

Scott, T. A., W. Wehtje, and M. Wehtje. 2001. The need for strategic planning in passive restoration of wildlife populations. Restoration Ecology 9:262-271.

Sherwood, W. L. 1895. The salamanders found in the vicinity of New York City, with notes upon extra-limital or allied species. Abstract of Proceedings of the Linnaean Society of New York 7:21-37.

Skelly, D. K., L.K. Freidenburg, and J. M. Kiesecker. 2002. Forest canopy and the performance of larval amphibians. Ecology 83:983-992.

Smith, E. 1899. The turtles and lizards found in the vicinity of New York City. Abstract of Proceedings of the Linnaean Society of New York 11: 11-32.

Smith, H. M., R. T. Zappalorti, A. R. Breisch, and D. I. McKinley. 1995. The type locality of the frog *Acris crepitans*. Herpetological Review 26 (1):14.

Stalter, R. 1996. Vegetation survey of Sagamore Hill NHS. xx pp., unpublished.

Stickel, L. F. 1951. Wood mouse and box turtle populations in an area treated annually with DDT for five years. Journal of Wildlife Management 15(2):161-164.

Unrine, J. M., C. H. Jagoe, W. A. Hopkins, and H. A. Brant. 2004. Adverse effects of ecologically relevant dietary mercury exposure in southern leopard frog (*Rana sphenocephala*) larvae. Environmental Toxicology and Chemistry. 23:2964-2970.

Weir, L. A., Royle A. J., Nanjappa, P., Jung, R. (2005): Modeling anuran detection and site occupancy on North American Amphibian Monitoring (NAAMP) routes in Maryland. Journal of Herpetology **39**: 627-639.

Williams, E. E., R. Highton, and D. M. Cooper. 1968. Breakdown of polymorphism of the red-backed salamander on Long Island. Evolution 22:76-86.

Windmiller, B. 1996. The pond, the forest, and the city: spotted salamander ecology and conservation in a human-dominated landscape. Ph.D. Dissertation, Tufts University, Boston, Massachusetts.

Wood, R. C., and R. Herlands. 1997. Turtles and tires: The impact of roadkills on Northern Diamondback Terrapin, *Malaclemys terrapin terrapin*, populations on the Cape May peninsula, southern New Jersey, USA. In: Proceedings: Conservation, Restoration, and Management of Tortoises and Turtles–an International Conference, p. 46-53i. Van Abbema, J. Ed., New York Turtle and Tortoise Society. New York, New York.

Yeaton, S. C. 1938. The reptilia of Long Island. Long Island Forum 1:4, 23-24.

Yeaton, S. C. 1968. The amphibians of Long Island. Sanctuary 1968 Summer:2-19. Long Island Chapter of the Nature Conservancy. Cold Spring Harbor, New York.

Yeaton, S. C. 1972. A natural history of Long Island. The Nature Conservancy, Long Island Chapter, Cold Spring Harbor, New York.

Ziminski, S. W. 1970. Notes on the decline of snakes at the Long Island Village of Hempstead and its vicinities. Engelhardtia 3: 2.

Zweifel, R. G. 1989. Long-term ecological studies on a population of painted turtles, *Chrysemys picta*, on Long Island, New York. Amererican Museum Novitates 2952:1-55.

NPS 419/105746 September 2010